Legal & Disclaimer

CONTENTS

CHARCOAL GRILLING 101: A GUIDE TO GETTING THAT PERFECT SEAR EVERY TIME

There's nothing like smell of a charcoal grill being fired up to get us salivating and ready to celebrate summer — but charcoal grilling can be intimidating. How do you start it? Where's the best spot for the food? When do you open the vents? Well, no need to worry — we've got you covered on the basics of grilling with charcoal.

How to start a charcoal grill

Traditional briquettes are inexpensive, light easily and burn long and steady. If you want a more intense, smoky flavor, go with hardwood charcoal (aka lump charcoal). These are blazingly hot but burn out faster.

Before you even light your grill, make sure to open to vents. The fire will need oxygen to keep going. After the charcoals are placed in the barbecue, you can control the internal cooking temperature by adjusting the vents: wider vents means hotter flames and more oxygen, while smaller vents means a cooler cooking temperature. Never close them all the way or the flames will go out.

Start your grill with a charcoal chimney; this is the easiest way to get your charcoal going. You do not need lighter fluid.

Stuff newspaper loosely in the bottom of the chimney (there is a space for it under the wire rack), then fill the chimney with charcoal. Remove top grate from grill, place chimney inside, and light the newspaper.

But how long should you let the coals burn? Let the charcoal or briquettes burn until they're covered with white-gray ash (it takes about 5 to 10 minutes for the coals to get to high heat and 25 to 30 minutes to get to medium heat).

Take the top grate of your grill off and, wearing protective grill gloves, hold the chimney by its handles and pour charcoal into the grill. Then take a paper towel soaked in vegetable oil, and spread it over grate with tongs. This is the trick to keep food from sticking to the grill.

What to grill on high heat

It takes about 5 to 10 minutes for the coals to get to high heat (about 700 degrees). Steaks, burgers and dense vegetables like corn on the cob and onions can handle high heat.

Grilling on high heat is the best way to get that perfect sear on the outside while keeping the inside juicy. To increase the temperature, open the vents to let in more oxygen. To decrease the temperature, close the vents — but not completely, or the fire will go out.

When grilling on high heat, create a two-fire zone: Stack more coals on one side of the grill for higher-temperature cooking, and the other side of the grill should have less charcoal for lower-temperature cooking. When grilling, sear foods on hot zone, then move over to cooler zone to cook through without burning.

After grilling, let the meat rest for five minutes on a cutting board. A board with a groove running around the perimeter is the perfect board since it collects all the juices the steak releases.

What to cook on medium heat

It takes about 25 to 30 minutes to get to grill to medium-heat temperature (about 500 degrees). Proteins that need to be thoroughly cooked through like pork chops, chicken, fish, uncooked hot dogs and sausages, along with denser fruits and vegetables like pineapple and eggplant, should be cooked on medium-heat.

Lots of medium-heat proteins use marinades (they will burn off on high heat). Marinate foods in a zip-top bag overnight — it fits easily in the fridge and fully envelops the meat. If you are short on time (you can't do it overnight), increase the amount of salt (things like soy sauce) and acid (things like citrus) to more quickly penetrate the meat, cutting down on time significantly.

What to grill on low heat

Christopher Arturo, Culinary Arts chef-instructor at the Institute of Culinary Education, does not recommend grilling at low heat (about 300 degrees) on a charcoal grill for the whole time because the protein will likely dry out. That being said, there are certain foods that do well cooked on high heat and then transferred to an area of the grill at low heat. Folks can do this with larger pieces of protein, like pork chops, as well as fattier fishes like salmon. Arturo also loves grilling a whole onion with this method.

How to clean a charcoal grill

Clean the grill right after cooking, while it's still hot, using a stiff-wire grill brush. Use it every time you grill to remove food particles from the cooking surface.

If you're looking for an alternative to using wire brushes (that may leave small wires and bits of metal behind), rub your grill grates with a peeled half onion," pitmaster Megan Day told TODAY Food. "Allow the grill to heat up to a high temperature. Pierce the half onion with a fork and rub the cut-side down along the grill grates. The onion's juices will release and produce steam to remove the bits and charred on debris."

BEEF

Aged Prime Rib

Servings: 8
Cooking Time: 120 Minutes

Ingredients:

- 2 tsp garlic salt
- 2 tsp onion salt
- 2 tsp kosher salt
- 1 tsp freshly ground black pepper
- 2 tsp dried rosemary
- 4lb (1.8kg) bone-in prime rib roast, aged for at least 28 days
- 3 garlic cloves, slivered
- 1/2 to 1 cup beef stock, as needed
- for the marrow butter
- 2 beef marrow bones, cut in half lengthwise at the butcher
- 1/2lb (225g) butter, softened
- 3/4 tsp chopped fresh flat-leaf parsley
- kosher salt and freshly ground black pepper
- to smoke
- hickory or oak wood chunks

Directions:

1. In a medium bowl, combine garlic salt, onion salt, kosher salt, pepper, and rosemary. Place roast in a baking dish and use a sharp knife to cut tiny slits every 2 inches (5cm), and insert the garlic slivers in the slits. Rub the roast with the spice mixture, cover with plastic wrap, and refrigerate for 24 hours.

2. Preheat the grill to 225°F (107°C). Once hot, add the wood chunks, install the heat deflector with a drip pan placed on top, and install a standard grate. Place roast and marrow bones on the grate, close the lid, and smoke until the internal temperature of the meat reaches 125°F (52°C), about 2 hours. Transfer roast to a large platter, cover with aluminum foil, and set aside to rest.

3. Remove the bones from the grill, and use a spoon to scrape the marrow from the bones into a medium bowl. To make the marrow butter, add butter and parsley to the marrow, and mix until well combined. Season with salt and pepper to taste. Set aside.

4. Remove the drip pan from the grill and pour the drippings into a medium all-metal saucepan. Place the saucepan on the heat deflector, close the lid, and heat for10 minutes, adding beef stock as needed. Season with salt and pepper to taste.

5. Place roast on a cutting board and slice. Serve immediately with the marrow butter and warm jus for dipping.

London Bridge London Broil

Servings: 4

Cooking Time: 10 Minutes

Ingredients:

- 1 (1 1/2 -2 pound) London Broil
- 1/2 tsp salt
- 1/4 tsp pepper
- 4 Tablespoons Herb Compound Butter

Directions:

1. Season both sides with salt and pepper.
2. Grilling:
3. Preheat the grill to 500°F using direct heat with a cast iron grate installed.
4. Place London Broil on the grid and close the dome for 3 minutes.
5. Flip the steak over and cook an additional 2 minutes.
6. Close all of the vents and let the steak sit for 5 minutes or until the internal temperature reaches 130°F.
7. Remove the steak and immediately top with dots of Herb Compound Butter.
8. Allow it to rest for 10 minutes before slicing thinly across the grain.

Mini Lamb Sliders With Tzatziki Sauce

Servings:6

Cooking Time: 12 Minutes

Ingredients:

- 11⁄2 lbs ground lamb
- 1 egg
- 2 tsp salt
- 1⁄2 tsp ground black pepper 2 cloves garlic (chopped)
- 1 tbsp chopped onion
- 1 tsp Italian seasonings
- 1 tsp Worcestershire sauce Mini pita pockets
- Arugula
- 1 cup plain Greek yogurt
- 1 cup sour cream
- 1 cup grated cucumber (peeled and seeded) 1 tsp salt
- 1⁄4 tsp pepper
- 2 cloves garlic (chopped)
- 2 tbsp lemon juice
- 1 tbsp fresh dill (chopped)
- 1 tsp olive oil
- 1⁄4 cup light brown sugar
- 1⁄4 cup brandy
- 1 small container Mascarpone
- 1 tbsp powdered sugar
- 6 slices Angel Food cake
- Maraschino cherries (optional for garnish)

Directions:

1. Preheat the grill to 450°F using direct heat with a cast iron grate installed.

2. Mix first 8 ingredients together and form small patties. Grill sliders in the BGE Slider Basket until done (about 2-3 minutes on each side). Open pita pockets and spoon in some Tzatziki sauce and add arugula. Add lamb sliders and enjoy!

3. Combine all ingredients and mix well. Refrigerate until ready to use.

4. Sprinkle pineapple slices with brown sugar on both sides. Let the slices sit for a few minutes. Grill pineapple for 2-3 minutes on each side or until pineapple slice becomes flexible. Remove from grid and place into a small bowl. Pour brandy on top of the pineapple; cool slightly and cut into quarters.

5. Combine powdered sugar and mascarpone and mix well. In the bottom of a martini glass layer, first the angel food cake, then the mascarpone, then the pineapple. Pour extra sauce into glasses. Garnish with pineapple slices and Maraschino cherries.

Herbed-up Prime Rib

Servings:8

Cooking Time: 150 Minutes

Ingredients:

- 1 (4-pound) bone-in standing rib roast
- Kosher salt and black pepper
- 4 tablespoons salted butter, at room temperature
- 1 tablespoon finely chopped fresh basil
- 1 tablespoon finely chopped fresh tarragon
- 1 tablespoon finely chopped fresh rosemary

Directions:

1. One hour before you plan to cook, take the roast out of the refrigerator. Preheat the grill to 350°F using direct heat with a cast iron grate installed. Season the roast on all sides with salt and pepper. In a small bowl, combine the butter, basil, tarragon and rosemary and mix well. Spread the herb butter all over the roast, applying the heaviest layer to the fat cap.

2. Place the roast, fat side up, on the kamado grill cooking grid and cook for about 2 hours, or until it reaches an internal temperature deep in the center of 125°F for medium-rare.

3. Transfer the roast to a platter, tent loosely with foil and let rest for at least 20 minutes or up to 30 minutes. Cut the meat away from the bones and slice the roast thickly or thinly against the grain as desired. Separate the leftover beef rib bones and serve them along with the meat.

Braised Short Ribs

Servings:8
Cooking Time: 130 Minutes

Ingredients:
- 8 bone-in beef short ribs
- 1 tsp salt
- 2 tsp freshly ground black pepper
- 4 tbsp olive oil
- ½ cup yellow onion, diced
- 3 cloves garlic, minced
- 1 cup beef broth
- 3 tbsp Worcestershire sauce
- 1 cup red wine
- 2 sprigs of rosemary

Directions:
1. Preheat the grill to 350°F using direct heat with a cast iron grate installed.
2. Season the short ribs with salt and pepper. Heat olive oil in the dutch oven. Sear short ribs for 1 minute per side. Remove from the dutch oven and set aside.
3. Add the onion to the dutch oven and cook for 3 minutes or until it is translucent. Add in garlic and cook for an additional minute.
4. Pour beef broth, Worcestershire sauce and red wine into the dutch oven. Bring to a simmer and add in the short ribs. Place the rosemary sprigs on top. Cover the dutch oven and cook for 2½ hours, or until meat is tender.

Smoked Oxtail Stew

Servings:6
Cooking Time: 240 Minutes

Ingredients:

- 3.5 lbs Oxtails
- 4 stalks celery, medium chopped
- 2 onions, medium chopped
- 8 oz cremini mushrooms, halved
- 1 small butternut squash, medium chopped
- 4 carrots, medium chopped
- Olive oil, salt, pepper (to brown)
- 6 tsp all purpose flour
- 3 tsp Louisiana Hot Sauce
- 1 tbs Creole seasoning
- 1 tbs granulated garlic
- 1 tbs fresh garlic
- 3 tbs whole grain dijon mustard
- 4 cups beef stock
- 2 tbs soy sauce
- 3 tbs ketchup
- 3 sprigs rosemary
- 2 x 14 oz cans chopped tomatoes
- 2 tbs salt
- 2 tbs pepper
- Mesquite and cherry wood, soaked in water
- Deep roaster foil pain (about 12" x 10" x 4")

Directions:

1. Oil, salt, and pepper the oxtails; brown on the grill with the cooking grid only. Let oxtails rest after browning.
2. Preheat the grill to 350°F using direct heat with a cast iron grate installed.
3. Cut all vegetables. Mix stock, mustard, soy, ketchup, and tomatoes in separate bowl. Place all vegetables, herbs, tails, and flour in a bowl and toss. Place mixture in a deep roasting pan and add liquid. Place soaked wood on fire and smoke for 4 hours at 350°F. Halfway through, cover with foil and stop adding wood.
4. After 4 hours, check tails for tenderness.
5. Enjoy with your favorite starch addition rice, potatoes, or pasta.

Snake River Farms Perfect Prime Rib

Servings:4

Cooking Time: 40 Minutes

Ingredients:
- Snake River Prime Rib
- Your favorite rub
- Salt & Pepper

Directions:
1. If the roast is frozen, put it in the fridge at least four days before you plan on cooking it. It will defrost naturally in cool temperatures over that time, which is ideal. If you don't have that kind of time, place the sealed roast in cool water to hasten the process.
2. Salt the roast on all sides the night before you plan to cook it. Leave it uncovered in your fridge overnight. This will look like it has dried out the roast, but it will actually increase the moisture in the prime rib when finished.
3. Remove the prime rib from fridge two hours before it is scheduled to go in the oven; allow it to come to room temperature. This will help the roast cook evenly.
4. Season the outside of your roast, using a pre-made rub, mix your own spices or just use salt and pepper. No matter what you use, sprinkle the seasonings generously.
5. Preheat the grill to 300°F using direct heat with a cast iron grate installed.
6. Place the prime rib in the center of the grill, fat side up. Cook for roughly 15-20 minutes per pound, removing the roast from the kamado grill when internal temperature reaches 110°F for rare, 120°F for medium rare and 130°F degrees for medium.
7. Let the roast rest for 20 minutes. In the meantime, remove your platesetter and setup your kamado grill for direct cooking at 500°F. Place the roast over direct heat for 90 seconds or until a crust forms on the outside of the roast.
8. Remove from heat, slice against the grain of the meat and serve immediately.

Red Gold Spicy Burgers

Servings:4
Cooking Time: 12 Minutes

Ingredients:
- 1 pound lean ground beef
- 1 (14.5 ounce) can Red Gold Petite Diced Tomatoes with Green Chilies, drained very well
- Salt and black pepper to taste
- For an added kick add a slice of pepper jack cheese into the center of each patty.
- Serve on toasted bun
- Top with Red Gold Mama Selita's Jalapeno Ketchup or Chipotle Mayo
- Top with slices of spicy peppers

Directions:
1. Preheat the grill to 400°F using direct heat with a cast iron grate installed.
2. Combine the ground beef and Red Gold Petite Diced Tomatoes with Green Chilies in a bowl. Form into patties and season with salt and black pepper.
3. Place directly on the cooking grid and cook for 5-6 minutes per side to desired temperature (160°F for completely cooked burgers).

North African Lamb Shoulder With Tomato Relish

Servings:6

Cooking Time: 180 Minutes

Ingredients:

- 2 tbsp coarse salt
- 2 tbsp black pepper
- 1 tbsp ground cumin
- 1 tbsp sweet paprika
- 1 boneless lamb shoulder, 5 to 6 lbs.
- ½ small sweet onion
- 3 large ripe tomatoes
- ½ tsp cumin
- 3 tbsp cilantro, chopped finely
- 2 tbsp fresh lemon juice
- 3 tbsp extra virgin olive oil
- Salt and pepper to taste

Directions:

1. Preheat the grill to 350°F using direct heat with a cast iron grate installed.
2. Combine the salt, pepper, cumin and paprika. Generously season the lamb with the spice mixture. Roll the lamb shoulder lengthwise into a compact roast and tie with butcher's string at 2-inch intervals.
3. Place the lamb on the cooking grid. Roast until the meat reaches an internal temperature of 180°F, about 3 hours.
4. Transfer the lamb to a cutting board and let it rest for 10 minutes; remove the string. Thinly slice the meat and arrange it on a platter and serve with the tomato relish.
5. While the lamb cooks, grate the onion into a mixing bowl with the coarse side of a box grater. Cut the tomatoes in half width and remove the seeds. Grate the tomatoes into the bowl. Stir in the cumin, cilantro, lemon juice, olive oil, and salt and pepper to taste.

Korean Short Ribs

Servings: 4

Cooking Time: 6 Minutes

Ingredients:
- 12 flanken style beef short ribs (about 4 lbs)
- 1 recipe Korean Barbecue Marinade

Directions:
1. Pour the marinade in a large zip top bag. Add short ribs. Seal and let sit in the fridge at least 4 hours, preferably overnight.
2. Remove short ribs from the oven before preheating the grill.
3. Grilling:
4. Preheat the grill to 500°F using direct heat with a cast iron grate installed.
5. Place the ribs directly on the grid and close the dome for 3 minutes.
6. Turn the ribs and cook an additional 2 minutes.
7. Remove the ribs, close all vents to extinguish the fire, and serve.

Barbecue Spare Ribs

Servings: 6
Cooking Time: 120 Minutes

Ingredients:

- 4 lbs boneless country style ribs
- 1/4 cup Basic Barbecue Rub
- 2 cups your favorite barbecue sauce (We like our Kansas City Barbecue Sauce)
- 2 Tablespoon olive oil

Directions:

1. Liberally season the country style ribs with the rub. Set aside.
2. Grilling:
3. Preheat the grill to 350°F using direct heat with a cast iron grate installed.
4. Heat the dutch oven on the stove with 2 Tablespoon of olive oil.
5. Brown each seasoned rib on all sides. Set aside.
6. Add ribs back into the pot along with barbecue sauce.
7. Cover the dutch oven and place on the grill.
8. Lower the dome for 2 hours.
9. Remove the dutch oven from the grill and serve.

Ny Strip Steaks

Servings:4

Cooking Time: 13 Minutes

Ingredients:

- 4 NY Strip steaks, seasoned with 4 tbsp Dizzy Gourmet Cosmic Cow Seasoning™
- 1 Tablespoon unsalted butter
- ¼ cup mushrooms, cut into bite size pieces
- ¼ cup chopped leeks
- 1 clove garlic, minced
- ½ cup whiskey
- 2 cups heavy cream
- ⅛ teaspoon cayenne pepper
- Salt and pepper

Directions:

1. Preheat the grill to 650°F using direct heat with a cast iron grate installed.
2. Grill steaks to desired internal temperature. 2 ½ minutes, then flip. 2 ½ minutes, then flip. Cook additional 3 minutes.
3. Set aside and keep warm.
4. Reduce heat to 350°F. Set a cast iron skillet or dutch oven on the grid and let it heat up for a few minutes. Add the butter and cook it until lightly brown, then add the mushrooms and cook until tender. Stir in leeks and garlic.
5. Slowly add the whiskey, it will ignite, so seriously, add it slowly! Once the whiskey burns off, stir and close the lid of the grill. Cook until the whiskey reduces by two-thirds. Add the cream, and stir frequently for 3 to 4 minutes. Add a little cayenne pepper and then add salt and pepper if you'd like.
6. Put the steaks on the grid and close the lid. Grill for about 4 minutes for medium-rare, turning once. Move the steaks to plates. Pour the sauce over the steaks and serve.

Jalapeño Brisket Flat

Servings:6

Cooking Time: 300 Minutes

Ingredients:

- 5 lb. brisket flat, with ½ inch fat cap left on
- 2 tbsp olive oil
- Ancho Chili & Coffee Seasoning
- 1 jar sliced jalapeños

Directions:

1. Preheat the grill to 300°F using direct heat with a cast iron grate installed.
2. Rub the brisket all over with the oil, then season it liberally on all of the exposed meat using Ancho Chili & Coffee Seasoning. Let rest for 15 minutes so the rub will adhere.
3. Place the brisket on the kamado grill fat side down and cook for 3 hours. After the brisket has cooked for 3 hours, place it in the pan, fat side down. Pour the jar of jalapenos over the brisket, juice and all, then place the pan back in the grill. Cook for 1 hour. Flip the brisket over and cover the pan tightly with aluminum foil. Cook for about 2 more hours until the brisket reaches an internal temperature of 205°F and is fork tender.
4. Remove the pan from the kamado grill and let rest for 15 minutes. Slice the brisket thinly against the grain and serve.

Bison, Mushroom And Roasted Veggie Stuffed Peppers

Servings:8

Cooking Time: 40 Minutes

Ingredients:

- 1 lb. Second City Prime ground bison
- 3-4 zucchini, cut lengthwise into ½ inch thick strips
- 2-3 whole medium carrots, washed and peeled
- 9 plum tomatoes, diced, or 1 28-ounce can of fire-roasted diced San Marzano-style tomatoes (drained)
- 2 tbsp extra virgin olive oil
- 2 tsp fresh or dried thyme + more for garnish (optional)
- 2 tsp fresh or dried basil + more for garnish (optional)
- 1 cup diced white onion
- 3 cloves of garlic, mined
- 1 8-ounce package of whole portabella mushrooms, washed and sliced
- 1 tsp crushed red pepper or chili flakes + more for garnish (optional)
- 2 cups cooked rice (we used yellow saffron rice for this recipe)
- 1 cup chicken stock
- 4-6 red, yellow or green bell peppers, tops cut off and seeds removed
- 5-6 mini tri-color peppers, tops cut off and seeds and stems removed
- 2 cups shredded sharp cheddar cheese
- ½ cup grated or shredded parmesan cheese
- Salt and coarsely ground black pepper to taste
- Fresh parsley minced for garnish (optional)

Directions:

1. Preheat the grill to 350°F using direct heat with a cast iron grate installed.

2. In a large bowl, toss the zucchini slices, carrots and tomatoes in 1 tablespoon of olive oil, plus 1 teaspoon each of thyme and basil. Salt and pepper to taste.

3. Add the remaining olive oil, diced onion, garlic and a pinch of thyme and basil – about ¼ tsp – to the cast iron skillet. Cook until the onion is translucent – about 2-4 minutes. Add the ground bison, breaking it down into smaller pieces as it cooks. While the bison is cooking add in the mushrooms and crushed pepper. Once the bison is cooked through, remove the skillet from the grill.

4. While the bison is cooling, place the zucchini, carrots and plum tomatoes directly on the perforated cooking grid and roast until tender – about 5 minutes. If you don't want to roast the plum tomatoes, you can use a can of diced fire roasted tomatoes as a quick alternative. Remove from the heat and let cool. Once the veggies have cooled, dice into small pieces.

5. In a large mixing bowl, add the bison mixture, rice, roasted diced veggies, 2 cups of diced tomatoes (or canned fire roasted tomatoes) and ½ cup of the chicken stock. Reserve the rest of the tomatoes to top the peppers. Add the rest of the herbs, salt and pepper to taste. Stir gently to incorporate ingredients.

6. Stuff the peppers with the bison rice mixture half way, then add a layer of 1 cup shredded cheddar cheese and finish stuffing to the top. Spoon the rest of the roasted tomatoes on top of each pepper. Place prepared raw peppers in dutch oven arranging the mini peppers between the large peppers. Cover bottom of dutch oven with the remaining chicken stock.

7. Place on grill, cover and cook for 30 minutes. Uncover and add a layer of the remaining shredded cheddar cheese to cover the top of the peppers and cook uncovered to melt the cheese. Once the cheese melts, remove from heat and let rest for 5 – 10 minutes.

8. Sprinkle peppers with parmesan cheese and garnish with crushed red pepper and herbs to taste. Transfer the peppers from the dutch oven to a plate or platter and serve.

Grape And Hatch Chile Marinated Tri Tip

Servings:6

Cooking Time: 75 Minutes

Ingredients:

- 3½ cups red, green and black Moscato grapes, rinsed
- 2 tablespoons whole grain Dijon mustard
- 1/3 cup white wine vinegar
- ¾ cup Cognac
- ½ sweet onion, diced
- 3 New Mexico Hatch Chiles, roasted; peeled; stemmed and seeded
- 1 lime, juiced
- 1 green apple, cored; diced
- Kosher salt and freshly ground pepper, to taste
- 1 Tri Tip Roast

Directions:

1. Preheat the grill to 350°F using direct heat with a cast iron grate installed.
2. Place the first 9 ingredients into a sauce pan and bring to a boil. Reduce the heat and simmer for 30 minutes. Remove from the heat and using an immersion blender, carefully purée the mixture.
3. Place the Tri tip in a resealable bag. Pour the marinade over the meat and seal the bag. Marinate for one hour.
4. After one hour, place the meat in the rectangular drip pan and pour the marinade over the top. Bake for 35-45 minutes or until you reach your desired doneness.

FISH AND SEAFOOD

Grilled Red Snapper With Tamari And Avocado

Servings:4
Cooking Time: 12 Minutes

Ingredients:

- 4 Tablespoon lemon juice
- 1 Tablespoon grated fresh ginger
- 1 Tablespoon fresh minced garlic
- 1 minced shallot
- 1 teaspoon honey
- 1 teaspoon tamari (soy sauce)
- 1 Tablespoon tahini
- 2 lbs. red snapper filets
- 1 large avocado

Directions:

1. Preheat the grill to 400°F using direct heat with a cast iron grate installed.
2. In heavy skillet, combine lemon juice, ginger, garlic, and shallot. Reduce by half over medium heat. In small bowl, combine honey, tamari, ½ cup water and tahini and whisk into lemon mixture. Set aside in warm place.
3. Broil or grill fish for 6 minutes on each side or until done. Serve with the warm sauce and garnish with avocado.

Red Chili Scallops

Servings:4
Cooking Time: 8 Minutes

Ingredients:
- 3⁄4 cup diced fresh mango
- 1⁄4 cup diced red bell pepper
- 1⁄4 cup diced red onion
- 1⁄4 cup thinly sliced scallions
- 2 tablespoons finely chopped fresh mint
- 1 clove garlic, crushed
- 2 tablespoons freshly squeezed lime juice
- 1 tablespoon extra-virgin olive oil
- 2 teaspoons honey
- 1⁄2 teaspoon kosher salt
- 1⁄4 teaspoon freshly ground black pepper
- 1 pound large sea scallops (12)
- 2 tablespoons Red Chile Rub
- 1 tablespoon cumin seed
- 1 tablespoon coriander seed
- 1 tablespoon red chile flakes
- 1 tablespoon ancho chile powder
- 1 tablespoon kosher salt
- 1 teaspoon sweet paprika
- 1 teaspoon garlic powder

Directions:

1. Set the kamado grill for direct cooking with the Cast Iron Grid.
2. Preheat the grill to 500°F using direct heat with a cast iron grate installed.
3. Using a wooden spoon, combine the mango, bell pepper, red onion, scallions, mint, garlic, lime juice, olive oil, honey, salt, and pepper in a small bowl and stir well. Set aside.
4. Season the scallops generously with the chili rub and place on the Grid. Close the lid of the kamado grill and grill the scallops for about 2 minutes on each side, or until golden and lightly cooked. Transfer the scallops to a platter.
5. To assemble the dish, place 3 scallops on each plate and top with 1/4 cup of the salsa. Serve immediately.
6. Toast the cumin seed, coriander seed, and chile flakes in a small skillet on the stovetop for about 5 minutes, or until fragrant. Remove from the heat and allow to cool.
7. Transfer the toasted spices to a spice grinder along with the chile powder, salt, paprika, and garlic powder. Grind for 15 to 20 seconds, until the spices are completely ground. Transfer to an airtight container until ready to use. Makes 1/2 cup.

Salt Baked Snapper

Servings:6

Cooking Time: 20 Minutes

Ingredients:

- 4 pounds Kosher salt
- 3 egg whites
- 1 whole snapper   (4-5 pounds cleaned)
- ¼ cup extra-virgin olive oil
- Lemon wedges

Directions:

1. Preheat the grill to 550°F using direct heat with a cast iron grate installed.
2. Mix salt and egg whites in a big bowl and mix until light and fluffy. Spread ¼ of the salt mixture on a thick pan covered with aluminum foil. Place cleaned fish onto the salt on the pan and cover with the rest of the salt mixture.
3. Place the dish in the grill and cook until internal temperature reaches 130°F. When done, let rest 10 minutes. Place fish on a platter and crack the salt crust with a hammer to reveal the tender fish.
4. Serve with grilled lemon wedges, fennel and herb salad drizzled with olive oil.

Florida Lobster Roll

Servings:6
Cooking Time: 28 Minutes

Ingredients:

- 4 tablespoons butter, divided
- Garlic powder
- 3 Florida lobster tails, about 7 ounces each
- ½ cup mayonnaise
- Zest from ½ of a Florida orange
- 1/3 cup finely chopped celery
- Pinch dried tarragon
- 6 hot dog buns, top split if available
- Slices of Florida avocado
- Spinach leaves

Directions:

1. Preheat the grill to 350°F using direct heat with a cast iron grate installed.
2. Split the top of the lobster shells and pull the meat out to rest on top. Cut a few slits in the meat so the lobster will cook evenly (you can have your fish monger do this for you). Place the tails on a perforated cooking grid and season lightly with salt and pepper.
3. Melt two tablespoons of butter and mix in a pinch of garlic powder. Brush the tails liberally with the butter. Place in the kamado grill and cook until the tails are firm to the touch, about 25 minutes; remove and let cool.
4. Remove the platesetter to cook direct at 350°F/177°C. Melt the remaining butter and mix in a pinch of garlic powder. Brush the sides of the rolls and grill them for 2 to 3 minutes on each side until golden brown. Remove the lobster meat from the shells and cut into large dice. Add to the dressing and mix well. Line each bun with a few spinach leaves. Lay a few slices of avocado in the bun and top each with an equal portion of the lobster mix.
5. Mix ingredients together in a large bowl.

Shrimp Boil

Servings: 4
Cooking Time: 40 Minutes

Ingredients:

- 1 1/2 lbs "easy peel" shrimp (this means the shrimp have been deveined, but the shells are still on)
- 1 lb baby red potatoes
- 2 Tablespoons butter
- 8 cloves garlic
- 6 sprigs fresh thyme
- 4 ears of corn, husked and snapped in half
- 2 lemons, halved
- 1/2 cup Old Bay seasoning
- Hot sauce and lemon wedges for garnish

Directions:

1. Preheat the grill to 450°F using direct heat with a cast iron grate installed with the dutch oven on the grid.
2. Fill the dutch oven with 4 quarts of water, lemons, thyme, garlic, and Old Bay seasoning and bring to a rolling boil with the lid on and the dome closed, about 20 minutes.
3. Lift the dome, remove the lid, and add potatoes.
4. Replace the lid and dome and cook for 10 minutes or until the potatoes are tender.
5. Add shrimp and corn and replace the lid and dome for an additional 5-7 minutes or until the shrimp are pink.
6. Transfer the shrimp and vegetables to a large bowl with a slotted spoon and toss with butter.
7. Serve with lemon wedges and hot sauce.

Whole Grilled Snapper In Pipian Sauce

Servings:10

Cooking Time: 76 Minutes

Ingredients:

- 2 whole snappers, cleaned, preferably with heads-on, each about 2 pounds
- Coarse salt, kosher or sea
- Freshly ground black pepper
- Lime, halved, for serving
- 1 sweet onion, peeled and thinly sliced
- 2 garlic cloves, peeled and thinly sliced
- 6 sprigs fresh cilantro
- 1 poblano chile (green or red), seeded and thinly sliced
- Extra virgin olive oil
- 8 fresh tomatillos, husked and rinsed
- 1 poblano pepper
- 3 serrano chiles
- ½ small onion
- 4 cloves garlic, peeled and skewered on a toothpick
- 2 scallions, trimmed
- 2 romaine lettuce leaves, cut into 1-inch slices
- 1 cup hulled pumpkin seeds
- ½ cup fresh cilantro, coarsely chopped
- 2 tbsp fresh flat-leaf parsley, coarsely chopped
- ½ tsp ground cumin
- 1 tbsp fresh lime juice, or more to taste
- 1 ½ cup water, or more as needed
- 2 tbsp extra virgin olive oil
- Sea salt and freshly ground black pepper to taste

Directions:

1. Preheat the grill to 450°F using direct heat with a cast iron grate installed.

2. Generously season the cavities of the fish with salt and pepper, then stuff with the onion, garlic, cilantro, and chile. Pin the cavities shut with toothpicks.

3. Brush the outside of the fish with olive oil, then make three diagonal, parallel slashes on the top side of each to facilitate even cooking.

4. Arrange the stuffed fish on the grill grate, slashed sides up.

5. Grill the fish until it is tender and the internal temperature is at least 145°F, 30 to 40 minutes, or as needed. Carefully transfer the fish to a platter using a wide spatula.

6. Preheat the grill to 500°F using direct heat with a cast iron grate installed.

7. Brush and oil the grill grate. Grill the tomatillos, poblano, serranos, onion, garlic, scallions, and lettuce leaves until golden brown, 2 to 4 minutes per side. Transfer to cutting board to cool to room temperature, then cut into 1-inch pieces.

8. Toast the pumpkin seeds in a dry cast iron skillet (not nonstick) over medium heat until they begin to brown and pop, 3 minutes. Shake the pan as the seeds cook; do not let them burn. Transfer the seeds to a shallow bowl to cool.

9. Set 3 tablespoons of seeds aside for a garnish, then grind the remaining seeds to a fine powder in a food processor, running the machine in short bursts. Work in 1/2 cup of water.

10. Place the grilled vegetables in a food processor and puree. Work in the cilantro, parsley, cumin, and lime juice. Work in an additional 1 cup water, adding more as needed to obtain a thick but pourable sauce.

11. Heat the olive oil in a large, deep skillet over medium heat. Add the pumpkin seed mixture and cook until dark, thick, and fragrant, about 5 minutes, stirring frequently to prevent splattering or scorching.

12. Stir in the tomatillo mixture and continue cooking the sauce until thick and richly flavored, 15 to 20 minutes, stirring often. Remove the sauce from the heat and taste for seasoning, adding salt to taste and/or more lime juice; the sauce should be highly seasoned. Set the sauce aside and keep it warm.

13. Spoon the Pipian Sauce over or under the fish. Sprinkle with the pumpkin seeds reserved from the sauce recipe. Serve with grilled limes halves for squeezing.

Grilled Shrimp And Taylor Farms Tangerine Crunch Wraps

Servings:2

Cooking Time: 6 Minutes

Ingredients:

- 1 lb. large shrimp, peeled and deveined
- Savory Pecan Seasoning
- 4-6 sundried tomato or spinach wraps
- 1 Taylor Farms Tangerine Crunch Chopped Kit
- bamboo skewers, soaked
- Feta cheese, optional

Directions:

1. Preheat the grill to 400°F using direct heat with a cast iron grate installed.
2. Season the shrimp on both sides with the   Savory Pecan Seasoning. Skewer the shrimp with the soaked skewers.
3. Place the shrimp on the kamado grill and cook for 3 minutes per side or until the shrimp are pink and firm. Remove from the grill, cool and remove from the skewers.
4. Heat a   plancha on the grill, griddle-side up.
5. Mix together the Taylor Farms Tangerine Crunch Chopped Kit. Fill the wrap with the salad, top with shrimp and feta cheese. Roll the wrap to enclose the salad. Heat the wrap on the plancha until you have your desired grill marks. Remove from the kamado grill and serve.

Sesame Tuna Flatbread

Servings:8

Cooking Time: 2 Minutes

Ingredients:

- 8 ounces Sushi grade tuna fillet
- 1 (8.5 ounce) package Naan bread
- 2 Tablespoons Better Than Bouillon Fish Base
- 1/4 cup sesame seeds
- 2 Tablespoons cracked black pepper
- 1 Tablespoon sweet chili sauce
- 3 (1/2") pineapple slices
- 1/4 cup sweet chili sauce
- 1/4 cup freshly chopped cilantro
- 1/2 cup cilantro leaves
- 1 teaspoon minced garlic
- 2 teaspoons Better Than Bouillon Fish Base
- 1 Tablespoon olive oil

Directions:

1. Preheat the grill to 425°F using direct heat with a cast iron grate installed. Place a nonstick grill pan onto the grid.
2. Mix the fish base, black pepper and sweet chili sauce in a small bowl. Coat the tuna and press with the sesame seeds.
3. Mix the sweet chili sauce   and cilantro together for the base. Set aside.
4. Mix the cilantro leaves, garlic, fish base and olive oil in a small bowl. Set aside.
5. Place the tuna and pineapple slices onto the grill pan and grill for 2 minutes per side. Add the Naan bread directly to the kamado grill. Grill for 1 minute per side. Slice the tuna into 1– 2 slices and cut the pineapple into 1/2 cubes.
6. Spread each Naan bread with half of the sweet chili base and sprinkle with 1 cup arugula. Add half of the tuna and pineapple to the top of the arugula and drizzle with the dressing. Serve immediately.

Blackened Grouper Sandwich

Servings: 4
Cooking Time: 12 Minutes

Ingredients:

- 4 skinless grouper fillets, about 6oz (170g) each
- 2 tbsp canola oil
- for the sauce
- 1/4 cup mayonnaise
- 1 1/2 tbsp sweet pickle relish
- 1 tbsp coarse ground mustard
- 1 tbsp ketchup
- for the seasoning
- 2 tsp onion powder
- 2 tsp garlic powder
- 2 tsp dried oregano
- 2 tsp dried basil
- 1 1/2 tsp dried thyme
- 1 1/2 tsp ground black pepper
- 1 1/2 tsp ground white pepper
- 1 1/2 tsp ground cayenne pepper
- 5 tsp paprika
- 3 tsp kosher salt
- to serve
- 4 hoagie rolls
- baby arugula
- tomato slices
- pickle spears

Directions:

1. Preheat the grill to 450°F (232°C) using direct heat with a cast iron grate installed and a cast iron skillet on the grate.

2. To make the sauce, in a medium bowl, combine mayonnaise, relish, mustard, and ketchup. Refrigerate until ready to serve.

3. To make the seasoning, in a small bowl, combine all the seasoning ingredients. Coat the fish fillets on all sides with the seasoning.

4. In the hot skillet, heat oil until shimmering. Place fish fillets in the skillet, close the lid, and cook until fish begin to form a crust, slightly char, and begin to flake, about 3 to 4 minutes per side.

5. Cut rolls in half, place on the grate, close the lid, and grill until grill marks appear, about 2 to 3 minutes.

6. Spread the sauce on the rolls. Place a fillet on each bottom bun, top with arugula and tomato, and close sandwiches. Serve immediately.

Bacon-wrapped Stuffed Shrimp

Servings:4
Cooking Time: 20 Minutes

Ingredients:
- 4 jumbo shrimp
- ¼ cup fresh crab meat
- 1 teaspoon olive oil
- ¼ teaspoon black pepper
- ¼ teaspoon red pepper
- ¼ teaspoon salt
- ¼ teaspoon parsley
- ¼ teaspoon lemon juice, fresh
- 4 slices of bacon
- 1 cup Italian dressing

Directions:
1. Preheat the grill to 350°F using direct heat with a cast iron grate installed.
2. Devein and butterfly the shrimp. Place the shrimp and Italian dressing in a freezer bag and marinate for at least 2 hours.
3. In a skillet, sauté the fresh crabmeat with olive oil, salt, black pepper, red pepper, parsley and lemon juice. Place a spoonful of the crabmeat in the shrimp and lay on the end of the bacon. Roll up the shrimp and bacon and fold it over to ensure crab meat stays intact. Place the shrimp on the Grid. Sear the bacon for a few minutes on each side. Cook for 20 minutes or until shrimp is pink.

Tuna Kabobs

Servings:2
Cooking Time: 10 Minutes

Ingredients:

- 2 tuna steaks, cut into 2-inch pieces
- 1 large red bell pepper, cut into 2-inch pieces
- 1 sweet onion, cut into 2-inch pieces
- 1 pineapple, cut into 2-inch pieces
- 1 cup Sweet Kentucky Bourbon Grilling Glaze
- Salt and pepper to taste

Directions:

1. Preheat the grill to 350°F using direct heat with a cast iron grate installed.
2. Thread the tuna, red bell peppers, onion and pineapple onto the skewers, leaving a small space between each item. Salt and pepper to taste.
3. Grill for 5 minutes then brush on the Sweet Kentucky Bourbon Grilling Glaze on both sides. Grill for another 5 minutes; glaze once more and remove from the kamado grill. Let rest for 10 minutes. Enjoy!

Grilled Shrimp And Linguica Skewers

Servings:4
Cooking Time: 18 Minutes

Ingredients:
- 2 each large Roma tomatoes
- 3 garlic cloves, roasted
- 1 tsp. salt
- ½ tsp. smoked paprika
- ¼ lb. unsalted butter, softened
- 2 tbsp. sherry vinegar
- 1 cup chopped fresh herbs (basil, parsley, cilantro, oregano)
- 1 tbsp. chopped capers
- 1 tsp. reserved juice from capers
- ½ tsp. lemon juice
- ¼ tsp. chili flakes
- 1 garlic clove, minced
- ¼ cup extra virgin olive oil
- 4 – 12" bamboo or metal skewers (bamboo soak in water for at least an hour)
- 16 each wild caught shrimp, U/12 size, head off, tail on, peeled and deveined
- 16 slices Linguica Sausage, ½"- ¾" thick
- 2 tbsp. blended olive oil or canola oil
- 4 tbsp. smoked tomato butter
- 2 tbsp. herb salsa verde
- Salt and pepper to taste

Directions:

1. Preheat the grill to 225°F using direct heat with a cast iron grate installed.

2. Cut the tomatoes in half; add to the grid and smoke tomatoes for 10 minutes until they are tender; set aside to cool.

3. Using a mortar and pestle or food processor, grind or process the roasted garlic, salt, smoked paprika and sherry vinegar into a paste. Mix the combination with the softened butter, and then grind the tomatoes together with the butter.

4. In a mixing bowl, combine all ingredients together and mix.

5. Preheat the grill to 375°F using direct heat with a cast iron grate installed.

6. Place a slice of Linguica sausage in the center of the shrimp; the shrimp will curl around the coin of sausage. Poke the skewer through the top of the shrimp, through the sausage and into the other end of the shrimp. The shrimp and sausage need to hold tightly on the skewer. Continue to complete the skewers, 2-3 shrimp and Linguica slices per skewer.

7. Brush the shrimp skewers lightly with oil and season with salt and pepper. Grill the skewers for approximately 6 minutes, turning them halfway through for desired grill markings and even cooking. Brush the skewers with the soft smoked tomato butter. Close the lid and cook for approximately 2 minutes.

8. With tongs, remove the skewers from the grill and spoon the herb salsa verde over the skewers.

Grilled Whole Trout

Servings: 2
Cooking Time: 20 Minutes

Ingredients:
- 2 whole trout (about 1 lb each), cleaned and gutted
- 2 Tablespoons olive oil
- 1/2 tsp salt
- 1/4 tsp pepper
- 4 cloves garlic, smashed
- 1/2 sliced lemon
- 1/2 bunch fresh parsley

Directions:
1. Brush the inside of the cavity and outside of the fish with olive oil and season with salt and pepper.
2. Stuff lemon, garlic, and parsley inside the cavity of each fish.
3. Grilling:
4. Preheat the grill to 400°F using direct heat with a cast iron grate installed.
5. Place the fish directly on the grid and close the dome for 10 minutes.
6. Gently flip the fish and close the dome for an additional 5-10 minutes or until the fish is cooked through.

Foil Packet Fish Filets

Servings: 4
Cooking Time: 15 Minutes

Ingredients:
- 4 (4 oz each) white fish filets
- 1/2 cup white wine
- 4 Tablespoons butter
- 4 pieces heavy duty foil
- 4 sprigs fresh thyme
- 4 green onions, cut in thirds
- 1 zucchini, julienned
- 1 large carrot, julienned
- 1 clove garlic, minced

Directions:
1. On the bottom of each foil sheet, place zucchini, carrot and onion to create a bed.
2. Place one fish filet on each bed of vegetables and top with garlic, thyme, 1 Tbs of butter, salt and pepper to taste.
3. Gather two sides of the foil together and fold down so the foil is almost touching the food.
4. Roll one side of the foil then pour in 2 Tablespoon of white wine. Close the remaining side. Repeat
5. Grilling:
6. Preheat the grill to 375°F using direct heat with a cast iron grate installed.
7. Place the foil packets on the grid and close the dome for 12-15 minutes or until the fish is cooked through.

POULTRY

Chicken & Dumplings

Servings: 4
Cooking Time: 95 Minutes

Ingredients:
- 1 Springer Mountain Farms whole chicken
- 2 quarts water
- 3 tsp salt
- ¼ tsp pepper
- 1 cup onion, chopped
- ½ cup celery, chopped
- 1 clove garlic, minced
- 8 oz. sour cream
- 2½ cups flour
- 3 eggs
- ½ cup water
- 2 tsp salt

Directions:
1. Preheat the grill to 325°F using direct heat with a cast iron grate installed.
2. Combine chicken, water, salt and pepper in dutch oven. Bring to a boil. Reduce heat; cover and simmer 1 hour. Remove chicken pieces; cut chicken into bite-size pieces, discarding skin and bones. Return chicken to broth along with onion, celery and garlic.
3. Cook 20 minutes. Add sour cream.
4. Combine flour, eggs (well beaten), water and 2 teaspoons salt and beat until batter is smooth. Drop batter by 1/2 teaspoon into boiling pot. Cover and simmer 15 minutes.

Chicken Pot Pie

Servings:4

Cooking Time: 40 Minutes

Ingredients:

- 3 cups frozen vegetable medley
- 1 lb. chicken thighs, boneless and skinless
- Savory Pecan Seasoning
- 1 cup white onion, diced
- 1 cup butter
- 1 cup flour
- 1 cup whole milk
- 1½ cups chicken stock
- Salt and pepper to taste
- 2 tbsp olive oil
- 2 pie crusts

Directions:

1. Preheat the grill to 425°F using direct heat with a cast iron grate installed.
2. Season the chicken thighs with Savory Pecan Seasoning and cook for 10 minutes per side, or until a 165°F internal temperature is reached. Chop the chicken and set aside to cool.
3. Preheat a Cast Iron Dutch Oven, then toss in the vegetables and sauté until they have a light char; set aside to cool. Add the butter and diced onion to the dutch oven and cook until translucent. Add the flour to create a roux; stir for 4 minutes then slowly add in the milk, followed by the stock, stirring consistently. Add in the chicken, vegetables and salt and pepper to taste.
4. Place the bottom pie crust into a greased pie pan and spoon in the filling. Cover with the top crust and crimp all the way around using your thumb and forefinger, being sure to seal the top and bottom together tightly. Using a paring knife make slits in the shape of a star in the center of the pie to allow steam to release. Cook for 30-35 minutes or until the crust is golden brown.

Rathbun Chicken

Servings:
Cooking Time: Minutes

Ingredients:
- 6 pound chicken
- Your favorite poultry seasoning
- Chicken thighs or breast
- Maple spice

Directions:
1. Preheat the grill to 325°F using direct heat with a cast iron grate installed.
2. In a roasting pan, season chicken by pouring spices inside the chicken and rubbing the outside as well.
3. Place chicken directly on the grid and cook to internal temperature of 172-175°F.
4. Place breast or thighs in the roasting pan and season with maple spices and place directly on the grid. Cook to same internal temperature as the whole chicken.
5. The chicken is ready when the juices run clear.

Hoisin Glazed Wings

Servings: 4

Cooking Time: 30 Minutes

Ingredients:

- 3-4 lbs chicken wings
- 1 cup Chinese Barbecue Sauce
- 1/4 cup Asian Rub

Directions:

1. Liberally dust the wings with the Asian Rub. Set aside.
2. Grilling:
3. Preheat the grill to 400°F using direct heat with a cast iron grate installed.
4. Place the wings on the grid with the dome closed for 20-30 minutes, turning once halfway through cooking.
5. When the juices run clear, place the wings in a large bowl and pour the Chinese Barbecue Sauce Sauce over them. Toss to coat.
6. Replace the wings on the grid and close all of the vents. Allow the wings to finish for 5 minutes.
7. Toss in the sauce once more and serve.

Rosemary Grilled Chicken Sandwiches

Servings:4
Cooking Time: 8 Minutes

Ingredients:

- 4 (4-ounce) boneless, skinless chicken breast halves, fat trimmed
- 3 tablespoons olive oil
- 2 tablespoons fresh lemon juice
- 1 tablespoon finely chopped fresh rosemary
- 2 teaspoons minced garlic (2 medium cloves)
- ½ teaspoon salt
- ¼ teaspoon freshly ground black pepper
- 8 slices Cabot Sharp Cheddar
- 4 ounces sliced Black Forest or other flavorful ham
- 4 buns, split
- Romaine leaves

Directions:

1. Place chicken between 2 large sheets plastic wrap; pound with mallet or heavy pan to flatten to even ½-inch thickness.
2. In medium bowl, whisk together oil, lemon juice, rosemary, garlic, salt and pepper; add chicken, turning to coat. Cover and refrigerate for about 1 hour.
3. Preheat the grill to 500°F using direct heat with a cast iron grate installed.
4. Remove chicken from marinade, shaking off excess. Cook on kamado grill until browned on outside and cooked through to center, 2 to 3 minutes per side. Toward end of cooking time, top each breast with slice of ham and cheese; cover with grill lid or foil until cheese is melted, about 2 minutes longer.
5. Serve on buns with bed of romaine leaves (toast buns on grill if desired).

Chicken & Veggie Stir-fry

Servings:6

Cooking Time: 10 Minutes

Ingredients:

- 2 tablespoons toasted sesame oil
- 1½ teaspoons plus 1½ teaspoons minced garlic
- 1½ teaspoons plus 1½ teaspoons minced fresh ginger
- 2 pounds boneless, skinless chicken breasts, cubed
- ½ cup rice wine
- ½ cup light soy sauce
- ½ cup chicken stock
- ¼ cup hoisin sauce
- 2 tablespoons rice wine vinegar
- 2 tablespoons granulated sugar
- 2 tablespoons cornstarch
- 1 teaspoon chili garlic sauce (optional)
- ½ cup canola oil
- 4 cups broccoli florets
- 1 cup broccoli stems, trimmed and julienned
- 1 cup julienned carrots
- 1 cup drained water chestnuts, diced
- 1 tablespoon toasted sesame seeds

Directions:

1. Preheat the grill to 500°F using direct heat with a cast iron grate installed.
2. Combine the sesame oil, 1½ teaspoons of the garlic, and 1½ teaspoons of the ginger in a small bowl, add the chicken, and toss to coat. Let the chicken marinate for 30 minutes.
3. To make the sauce, mix the remaining 1½ teaspoons garlic, 1½ teaspoons ginger, rice wine, soy sauce, chicken stock, hoisin sauce, rice wine vinegar, sugar, cornstarch, and chili garlic sauce in a small bowl. Set aside.
4. Place a Carbon Steel Wok on the spander and preheat for 2 minutes.
5. Place the canola oil and chicken in the wok. Close the lid of the kamado grill and cook for 5 to 6 minutes, until seared on all sides. Add the broccoli florets and stems, carrots, and water chestnuts and cook for 2 to 3 minutes, stirring well. Add the sauce and continue to cook until the sauce has thickened. Remove the wok from the kamado grill.
6. Transfer the stir-fry to a bowl and garnish with the sesame seeds.

Salsa Verde Chicken Pasta

Servings:6
Cooking Time: 45 Minutes

Ingredients:

- 3 boneless, skinless chicken breasts, cubed
- 1½ tbsp olive oil
- 3 tomatillos, chopped
- 1 large white onion, chopped
- 1 large red bell pepper, chopped
- 1½ tsp paprika
- Salt and pepper to taste
- 3 cups uncooked rigatoni or rotini pasta
- 2¼ cups chicken broth (low sodium)
- 1½ cups salsa verde
- 4 tbsp chopped cilantro (save more for garnish)
- 5 ounces cream cheese
- 1 lime, juiced
- Diced avocado for topping

Directions:

1. Preheat the grill to 350°F using direct heat with a cast iron grate installed.
2. Preheat a Cast Iron Skillet for 5 minutes. Add the olive oil, tomatillos, onions and peppers and cook for 5 minutes, stirring occasionally.
3. Season the chicken with the paprika, salt and pepper; add to the skillet and cook for another 5 minutes.
4. Add the uncooked pasta, broth, salsa and cilantro. Cook for 25-30 minutes until the pasta is cooked through and the liquid is reduced; swirl in the cream cheese until melted. Remove from the kamado grill and stir in the lime juice.
5. Top with diced avocado and cilantro

Amusement Park Turkey Legs

Servings: 4
Cooking Time: 240 Minutes

Ingredients:

- 2 fresh turkey drumsticks
- 4 cups Turkey Brine
- 2 cups apple or cherry wood chips, soaked in water for 30 minutes

Directions:

1. Submerge drumsticks into the turkey brine for as few as 2 hours and as long as overnight.
2. Remove the drumsticks and discard the brine. Pat the turkey dry.
3. Grilling:
4. Preheat the grill to 250°F using direct heat with a cast iron grate installed. Add soaked, drained wood chips to the burning coals.
5. Put the plate setter in place and place the grid on top.
6. Place the turkey legs on the grid and close the dome for 3-4 hours or until the turkey registers 170°F.
7. Remove the drumsticks and pretend to walk around an amusement park or renaissance fair

Turkey & Wild Mushroom Pot Pie

Servings:4

Cooking Time: 55 Minutes

Ingredients:

- 1½ cups mixed dried wild mushrooms
- 2 Tbsp unsalted butter
- 2 Tbsp olive oil
- 1 cup diced onions
- 1 cup diced carrots
- 1 cup diced celery
- 2 Tbsp minced garlic
- ⅓ cup all-purpose flour
- ¼ cup white wine
- 3 cups low-sodium chicken stock
- 1 cup diced potatoes
- 1 tsp minced fresh thyme
- 1 cup frozen green peas
- 2 cups chopped roasted turkey breast
- 1 (9-inch) deep-dish pie shell and 1 pie dough disk
- 1 large egg
- 1 tablespoon water

Directions:

1. Preheat the grill to 375°F using direct heat with a cast iron grate installed. Place the Dutch Oven on the grid to preheat for 10 minutes.

2. Cover the mushrooms with hot water and let rehydrate until needed. Heat the butter and olive oil in the Dutch Oven. Add the onions, carrots, and celery. Close the lid of the kamado grill and cook uncovered for 5 to 6 minutes, until the vegetables are light brown and softened. Add the garlic and stir for 1 minute, then add the flour and stir. Add the wine and cook for 3 minutes.

3. Drain the mushrooms, reserving the liquid. Add the chicken stock and the reserved mushroom liquid to the Dutch Oven and stir well. Add the potatoes. Close the lid of the kamado grill and continue cooking, covered, for 10 minutes, or until the potatoes are cooked through. Add the reserved mushrooms, thyme, peas, and turkey, stir, and cook for 2 to 3 more minutes. Remove the Dutch Oven from the heat and let cool for 15 minutes.

4. Using the Grill Gripper and barbecue mitts, carefully remove the grid and add the platesetter. Replace the grid and raise the kamado grill temperature to 400°F.

5. Spoon the filling into the pie shell. Roll out the pie dough disk on a lightly floured surface until it is large enough to cover the top of the pie. Unroll the pie dough onto the pie. Press the top and bottom edges of the dough together and crimp. Using a knife, cut four small slits on the top of the crust. Beat the egg with the water and brush the top with the egg wash.

6. Place the pie on top of the grid and close the lid of the kamado grill. Cook for 30 to 40 minutes, until the dough is light brown and the filling is hot and bubbling. Let rest for 5 minutes before serving.

Rotisserie Chicken

Servings: 6
Cooking Time: 90 Minutes

Ingredients:

- 1 (4-5 lb) whole chicken, gizzards and giblets removed
- 2 quarts warm water
- 1/4 cup kosher salt
- 1/4 cup brown sugar
- 2 Tablespoons whole peppercorns
- 1 lemon, halved
- 2 lbs small waxy potatoes, cut in half (we like Yukon golds)
- 1 lbs carrots, cut into 2 inch chunks
- 1/4 cup butter, softened
- 1 onion, cut into wedges
- 2 sprigs fresh thyme
- 4 whole cloves garlic

Directions:

1. Combine brine ingredients until the salt and sugar dissolve and add enough ice to bring the brine to room temperature.
2. Submerge the chicken into the brine and allow to chill in the refrigerator for a minimum of 2 hours and up to overnight.
3. Remove the chicken from the brine and pat dry.
4. In the bottom of a cold dutch oven, place the vegetables and top with the chicken, breast side up.
5. Gently lift the skin away from the meat and rub butter beneath the skin.
6. Grilling:
7. Preheat the grill to 425°F using direct heat with a cast iron grate installed.
8. Cover the dutch oven and place on the grill. Lower the dome for 1-1 1/2 hours or until the internal temperature of the meatiest part of the thigh registers 160°F
9. Remove the dutch oven from the grill and allow it to sit for an additional 10 minutes before removing the lid.
10. Remove the chicken, place the vegetables on a platter or in a bowl. Carve the chicken and serve.

Open-faced Leftover Turkey Sandwich

Servings:4

Cooking Time: 14 Minutes

Ingredients:

- Sourdough bread
- 3 tsp butter, separated
- Mashed potatoes
- Stuffing or dressing
- Gravy
- Roasted turkey
- Cranberry chutney or cranberry sauce
- Salt and pepper to taste
- Arugula, optional

Directions:

1. Preheat the grill to 400°F using direct heat with a cast iron grate installed.
2. Melt one tablespoon of butter in the cast iron skillet or plancha and add the mashed potatoes. Once they have a nice crust remove and set aside. Next, add the stuffing with gravy and a tablespoon of butter. Once warmed, about 5-7 minutes, remove and set aside. Lastly, add the turkey with more gravy. Once warmed, about 5-7 minutes, remove and set aside.
3. Toast the bread with a tablespoon of butter and salt and pepper. Then pile on the cranberry chutney or sauce! Next, comes the turkey. Follow it up with the mash potatoes and stuffing. Then drizzle more gravy over. Top with arugula and serve immediately.

The Perfect Roasted Turkey

Servings:4
Cooking Time: 12 Minutes

Ingredients:

- 1 turkey, cleaned thoroughly
- poultry seasoning
- 1 whole onion cut in half
- 1 stalk celery
- 2 cups chicken broth, wine or water

Directions:

1. Preheat the grill to 325°F using direct heat with a cast iron grate installed. Use a handful of pecan chips for a light, smoky flavor and to provide a deep brown color to the turkey.
2. Spread the seasoning generously over the outside of the bird. Load the bird onto a Vertical Poultry Roaster or Rib and Roasting Rack, then place into a drip pan. Add the onion and celery to the drip pan. Fill the pan with chicken broth, wine, or water.
3. Cook for 12 minutes per pound until the turkey has reached a safe minimum internal temperature of 165°F throughout the product. Reserve the drippings from the drip pan to make gravy.

Smoked Turkey

Servings:8
Cooking Time: 38minutes

Ingredients:

- 12-14 lb. whole turkey
- Sweet and Smoky Seasoning
- Canola oil
- Kosher salt
- ½ orange, cut in half
- ½ onion, cut in half
- 2 sprigs sage
- 2 sprigs rosemary
- 2 sprigs thyme
- 1 whole head of garlic

Directions:

1. Preheat the grill to 225°F using direct heat with a cast iron grate installed.
2. Coat the turkey in canola oil and place on rib rack inside of the roasting pan. Season with salt and sweet and smoky seasoning making sure to season the cavity as well. Put orange, onion, garlic and herbs into the cavity.
3. Smoke in the kamado grill until the internal temperature of the breast meat is 165ºF, the dark meat will be about 185ºF internal temperature. Typically, it is about 30 minutes per lb., between 6 to 8 hours.
4. Let rest for 15 minutes, and serve!

Polynesian Duck Kabobs

Servings:8

Cooking Time: 15 Minutes

Ingredients:

- 6- 7.5 oz Maple Leaf Farms Boneless Duck Breast Filets, thawed if frozen
- Salt and fresh ground black pepper, to taste
- 1 ripe fresh pineapple, peeled and cored
- 2 large red or yellow bell peppers, or one of each
- 2 large green bell peppers
- 2 small red onions
- 2/3 cup pineapple preserves
- 3 tablespoons dijon mustard

Directions:

1. Preheat the grill to 350°F using direct heat with a cast iron grate installed.
2. Remove skin from duck breasts. Cut duck breast into 2 inch chunks; season with salt and pepper to taste.
3. Cut pineapple into 1½ inch chunks. Cut bell peppers into 1½ inch chunks, discarding stems and seeds. Cut onions through the core into ½ inch thick wedges. Alternately thread duck, pineapple, bell peppers and onions onto Flexible Skewers.
4. Combine preserves and mustard; mix well. Arrange duck kabobs on kamado grill. Brush half of preserve mixture over kabobs. Grill covered 5 minutes. Turn; brush remaining half of preserve mixture over kabobs. Continue grilling covered 5 to 6 minutes or until duck is barely pink in center and peppers are crisp-tender.

PORK

Championship Ribs

Servings:2
Cooking Time: 90 Minutes

Ingredients:

- 3 slabs of St. Louis-style ribs or baby back ribs, cut in half, membrane off* and ribs washed
- 1 cup of your favorite commercial or homemade dry BBQ rub
- 1 cup honey
- 1-1/2 cups apple juice
- 2 cups honey BBQ Sauce
- 1/2 cup salt
- 1/2 cup turbinado sugar
- 1/4 cup granulated brown sugar
- 1 tbsp granulated garlic
- 1 tbsp granulated onion
- 2 tbsp paprika
- 2 tbsp chili powder
- 2 tbsp freshly ground black pepper
- 2 tsp cayenne
- 1 tbsp thyme leaves
- 1 tbsp ground cumin
- 1 tsp ground nutmeg

Directions:

1. Cover the ribs with the rub, using about two-thirds on the meaty side and one-third on the boney side. Allow to stand at room temperature for 30 minutes before grilling.
2. Preheat the grill to 325°F using direct heat with a cast iron grate installed. Using a handful of hickory and cherry chips will help carmelize the ribs.
3. Cook for one-and-a-half hours, using a rib rack if you need it to have sufficient space for three slabs of ribs. Remove ribs to a flat pan or cookie sheet and brush them all on both sides with honey.
4. Put the ribs in an aluminum foil pan with about one-inch of apple juice in the bottom, standing them on end in the pan if necessary to get them to fit. Cover with foil and continue cooking for about one hour, replenishing the apple juice if needed to maintain liquid in the pan. Test the ribs by inserting a toothpick to determine whether they are tender.
5. At this point, you could cool them down, wrap each slab separately and refrigerate them for a day or two. They can then be transported to a tailgate party or reheated for entertaining at home.
6. When ready to serve them, transfer the cooked ribs to a medium hot grill. Brush with Honey BBQ Sauce; heat a few minutes, flipping them to heat both sides. Cut in to pieces and serve.
7. Removing the membrane: Carefully slide an implement, such as a fish skinner (available in the sporting goods department), the tip of a butter knife or the tip of a meat thermometer between the membrane and a bone near the end of the rack of ribs. Rock the implement back and forth gently to loosen the membrane until you have enough space to slide your finger under it. Using a paper towel, pull up the membrane and slowly peel the membrane off.
8. Combine all ingredients, mix well, and store in an airtight container.

Turkey Bacon Dogs

Servings:8
Cooking Time: 20 Minutes

Ingredients:

- 8 Nature's Own 100% Whole Wheat Hot Dog Rolls
- 1 package (16 ounces) Butterball Bun Size Premium Turkey Franks
- 8 slices Butterball Turkey Bacon
- 1/2 to 3/4 cup shredded Cheddar or Monterey Jack cheese
- Salsa (medium or hot)
- Pickled jalapeño pepper slices (optional)
- Sour cream (optional)

Directions:

1. Preheat the grill to 500°F using direct heat with a cast iron grate installed.
2. Spray cold grate of grill with cooking spray. Wrap each turkey frank with 1 slice turkey bacon. Grill franks, turning frequently, until bacon is crisp.
3. Place franks in hot dog rolls. Immediately sprinkle with cheese. Serve with salsa and if desired, jalapeno pepper slices and sour cream.

Potato Salad With Bacon

Servings:6
Cooking Time: 20 Minutes

Ingredients:

- 6 slices bacon, thick-cut, cooked until crisp, then coarsely crumbled
- 2 pounds red new potatoes, (golf-ball size), scrubbed and poked with a fork
- 2 tablespoons extra-virgin olive oil
- 4 green onions, including green tops, cut crosswise into thin rounds
- ¼ cup extra-virgin olive oil
- 1 tablespoon apple cider vinegar
- 1 large clove garlic, minced
- 2 tablespoons fresh parsley, minced
- 1 teaspoon kosher salt
- ½ teaspoon sugar
- 1 teaspoon freshly ground black pepper

Directions:

1. Preheat the grill to 350°F using direct heat with a cast iron grate installed.
2. In a medium bowl, toss potatoes with olive oil until well coated. Arrange potatoes around outer edges of cooking grid. Grill until tender when pierced with a knife, about 20 minutes.
3. While potatoes are grilling, put green onions and bacon in a large bowl, and make dressing. Combine olive oil, vinegar, garlic, parsley, salt, sugar and pepper in a small bowl; set aside.
4. When potatoes are tender, transfer to a cutting board and cool for 5 minutes. Cut potatoes in half and add to bacon and onions in the bowl. Stir dressing to combine and pour over potatoes. Gently toss to thoroughly combine. Serve immediately.
5. The potato salad can be made up to 2 hours prior to serving. Cover and set aside at room temperature.

Barbecued Pork Shoulder With Carolina Sauce

Servings:12

Cooking Time: 660 Minutes

Ingredients:
- 1 whole bone in pork butt, about 8 pounds
- 2 tbsp olive oil
- Savory Pecan Seasoning
- 1/2 cup apple juice
- Bold and Tangy Carolina Barbecue Sauce

Directions:
1. Preheat the grill to 275°F using direct heat with a cast iron grate installed.
2. Trim any loose fat from the butt but leave the heavy fat cap on. Rub the butt all over with the oil and season the butt liberally on all the meaty surfaces with the   Savory Pecan Seasoning.
3. Place the butt on the kamado grill fat side down. Cook for about 8 hours until it reaches an internal temperature of 170°. Lay out a big sheet of double thick heavy-duty aluminum foil and put the pork butt in the middle. fat side up. As you begin to close up the package pour the apple juice in the bottom and then seal the package. Put the butt back in the kamado grill and cook until it reaches an internal temperature of 200° deep in the meaty part. This should take another 2 to 3 hours.
4. When the pork is done remove it from the kamado grill and open the package. Let cool for 15 minutes. With meat claws pull the pork apart discarding any fat or bones. Top it with the   Bold and Tangy Carolina Barbecue Sauce or   Vidalia Onion Sriracha Barbecue Sauce and toss to combine. Serve with sauce on the side.

Pulled Pork Baked Beans

Servings:6
Cooking Time: 60 Minutes

Ingredients:

- 3 cans Navy beans (drained and rinsed)
- 1 lb. pulled pork
- ¾ cup chicken stock
- 2 tsp kosher salt
- 3 tbsp   Sweet & Smoky Kansas City Style BBQ Sauce
- 2 tbsp   Vidalia Onion Sriracha BBQ Sauce

Directions:

1. Preheat the grill to 350°F using direct heat with a cast iron grate installed.
2. Into the dutch oven, add beans, pork, chicken stock, salt, and BBQ sauces. Let simmer for 45 min to an hour.
3. Let cool for 5-10 minutes, serve and enjoy!

Reverse-seared Herb Crusted Bone-in Iberico Pork Loin

Servings:10

Cooking Time: 65 Minutes

Ingredients:

- 1 2.5-lb. bone-in pork loin
- 2 tbsp minced rosemary
- 2 tbsp minced oregano
- ¼ cup minced sage
- 2 tbsp minced thyme
- 6 cloves minced garlic
- 4 tbsp kosher salt
- 2 tbsp ground black pepper
- ½ cup Dijon mustard

Directions:

1. Set the kamado grill with the platesetter basket with one side indirect cooking (with the Half Moon Pizza & Baking Stone) and the other side preheat the grill to 300°F using direct heat with a cast iron grate installed.
2. Mix all ingredients for the crust in a bowl, and coat the pork loin with the crust. Place the roast on the indirect side of the kamado grill and roast for about 40 minutes. A good rule of thumb is to roast the pork for 20 minutes per pound. Once the internal temperature reaches 135°F move the pork loin to the direct side of the grill. Sear the pork for about 5 minutes per side or until the internal temperature is 145°F.
3. Let rest for 10 minutes, slice in between the bones and serve with your preferred sides.

Hoppin' John

Servings:10
Cooking Time: 35 Minutes

Ingredients:
- 4 Tbsp butter
- 1 whole medium yellow onion, chopped
- 4 cloves garlic, minced
- 1 whole green pepper, diced
- 2 stalks celery, diced
- 4 cups black-eyed peas, soaked at least 6 hours
- 5 cups chicken broth
- 1 ham hock
- Salt and pepper, to taste
- ½ tsp cayenne pepper
- ½ tsp basil
- ¼ tsp thyme
- ¼ tsp oregano
- 1 bay leaf
- 2 Tbsp white vinegar
- 4 cups white rice, cooked

Directions:
1. Preheat the grill to 350°F using direct heat with a cast iron grate installed.
2. Heat butter in a   cast iron Dutch Oven. Add onion, garlic, green pepper, and celery. Cook for 5 minutes. Stir in soaked black-eyed peas, chicken broth, ham hock, salt and pepper, cayenne, basil, thyme, oregano and bay leaf. Cook for 30 minutes.
3. Stir in vinegar. Serve over the cooked rice.

Bourbon Glazed Pork Tenderloin

Servings:4

Cooking Time: 13 Minutes

Ingredients:
- 1 teaspoon smoked paprika
- 1/4 teaspoon cinnamon
- 1 teaspoon salt
- 2 teaspoons olive oil
- 1/2 cup peach preserves
- 2 tablespoon bourbon
- 2 (1-pound) pork tenderloins, trimmed and silver skin removed
- 5 peaches, unpeeled and cut into quarters

Directions:
1. In a small bowl, combine paprika, cinnamon and salt. Rub tenderloins with olive oil and sprinkle with spice rub.
2. Preheat the grill to 400°F using direct heat with a cast iron grate installed. Grill pork, turning as needed, until lightly charred and meat thermometer inserted in thickest part registers 135°F, about 9 minutes. During the last few minutes of grilling, brush pork with peach glaze to finish.
3. While pork is grilling, place peach quarters on kamado grill for about 2 minutes per side, until lightly charred. Allow pork to rest 10 minutes before slicing. Serve with grilled peaches.

Pork Crown Roast

Servings:8
Cooking Time: 120 Minutes

Ingredients:
- 2 7-boned, frenched sections of pork loin
- ½ cup Dijon mustard
- 1 pound ground pork-sage sausage
- 8 cups quartered small white mushrooms
- 2 cups diced yellow onions
- 1 cup diced celery
- 1 cup peeled and diced Granny Smith apple
- 1 cup chicken stock
- 1 large egg, beaten
- 4 cups plain croutons

Directions:
1. Preheat the grill to 350°F using direct heat with a cast iron grate installed.
2. Watch the video to learn to work the pork loin sections into a crown.
3. Using a basting brush, cover the crown roast, both inside and outside, with the mustard and set aside. Brown the sausage, mushrooms, onions, celery, and apple in a dutch oven until caramelized. Using a slotted spoon, transfer the mixture to a medium bowl and let cool. Stir the chicken stock and the beaten egg together in a large bowl, add the croutons and continue to mix. Add the sausage mixture to the croutons and combine until all the ingredients are thoroughly blended.
4. Put the stuffing in the center of the pork crown roast and cover the top of the roast with aluminum foil. Place the roast on the grid above the Roasting & Drip Pan and close the lid of the grill. Cook for 1½ hours. Remove the foil, close the lid of the grill, and cook for 30 to 45 minutes longer, until the internal temperature of the pork registers 145°F. Remove the roast from the heat and let rest for 15 minutes. Slice and serve.

Pork, White Bean & Kale Soup

Servings: 6

Cooking Time: 40 Minutes

Ingredients:

- 1 tbsp extra virgin olive oil
- 1lb (450g) pork tenderloin, trimmed and cut into 1-in (2.5-cm) pieces
- 3⁄4 tsp kosher salt
- 1 medium yellow onion, finely diced
- 4 garlic cloves, minced
- 2 tsp smoked paprika
- 1⁄4 tsp crushed red pepper flakes (optional)
- 1 cup dry white wine
- 4 Roma tomatoes, chopped
- 4 cups low-sodium chicken stock
- 1 bunch of kale, ribs removed and leaves chopped
- 15oz (425g) can white beans, drained and rinsed
- crusty French bread, to serve

Directions:

1. Preheat the grill to 300°F (149°C) using indirect heat with a dutch oven on the heat deflector. In the hot dutch oven, heat oil until shimmering. Add pork pieces and sprinkle with salt. Close the grill lid and cook until pork is no longer pink on the outside, about 2 minutes, stirring once or twice. Transfer pork to a bowl, leaving the juices in the dutch oven.

2. Return the dutch oven to the grill and add the onion. Close the grill lid and cook until beginning to brown, about 2 to 3 minutes, stirring a few times. Add garlic, paprika, and red pepper flakes (if using), close the grill lid, and cook until fragrant, about 30 seconds, stirring once or twice. Add wine and tomatoes, and stir to scrape up any browned bits. Add stock, close the lid, and heat until beginning to simmer, about 5 to 10 minutes.

3. Once simmering, add kale and stir until wilted, about 5 to 8 minutes. Close the top and bottom vents to reduce the heat, and simmer until kale is tender, about 5 to 8 minutes more, stirring occasionally. Stir in beans, reserved pork, and any accumulated juices. Simmer until beans are heated and pork is fully cooked, about 2 to 5 minutes. Remove the dutch oven from the grill, and serve immediately with crusty bread.

Sweet & Spicy Pulled Chicken

Servings: 10
Cooking Time: 120 Minutes

Ingredients:
- 2 whole chickens, about 4lb (1.8kg) each
- for the brine
- 1/2 cup kosher salt
- 1/2 cup packed light brown sugar
- 3 tbsp pickling spice
- 6 cups hot water
- for the rub
- 4 tbsp paprika
- 2 tbsp ground black pepper
- 4 tsp ground cayenne pepper
- 2 tbsp raw sugar
- 2 tbsp kosher salt
- for the sauce
- 1 cup bourbon
- 4 tbsp molasses
- 3 cups cider vinegar
- 2 cups water
- 4 chipotle peppers in adobo sauce, chopped
- 4 tbsp kosher salt
- 2 tbsp crushed red pepper flakes
- 2 tbsp ground black pepper
- 4 tsp ground cayenne pepper
- to smoke
- peach, plum, or grapevine wood chunks

Directions:

1. To make the brine, in a large bowl, whisk together all the brine ingredients until salt and sugar have dissolved. Add ice cubes a few at a time until the liquid is no longer hot. Place each chicken in a resealable plastic bag and add brine to cover. (Any extra brine can be refrigerated and saved for a later use.) Refrigerate for 6 to 24 hours.

2. To make the rub, in a small bowl, combine all the rub ingredients. Remove chicken from the brine and pat dry with paper towels. Cover all the surfaces with the rub, wrap tightly with plastic wrap, and allow to come to room temperature.

3. To make the sauce, in a large saucepan, combine all the sauce ingredients. Place pan on the stovetop over high heat, bring to a simmer, and cook for 5 minutes.

4. Preheat the grill to 275°F (135°C). Once hot, add the wood chunks and install the heat deflector and a standard grate. Place chicken on the grate breast side up, close the lid, and smoke until the meat of the thigh reaches an internal temperature of 170°F (77°C), about 60 to 90 minutes, basting with sauce every 15 to 20 minutes. Remove chicken from the grill and let rest for 20 minutes.

5. On the stovetop in a small saucepan over high heat, boil any remaining basting sauce for 5 minutes. Remove the meat from the bones and shred. Toss the shredded chicken with the warmed basting sauce and serve immediately.

Pomegranate Pork Roast

Servings: 6
Cooking Time: 60 Minutes

Ingredients:

- 1 (5 lb) pork loin roast
- 1/2 cup pomegranate molasses
- 2 Tablespoons fresh rosemary, minced
- 1 Tablespoon hot Chinese mustard
- 1 tsp salt
- 1/2 tsp pepper
- 4 cloves garlic, minced

Directions:

1. In a small bowl, combine molasses, mustard, garlic, and rosemary..
2. Pat the pork loin roast dry and season with salt and pepper.
3. Grilling:
4. Preheat the grill to 500°F using direct heat with a cast iron grate installed and place the plate setter and grid inside.
5. Set the pork roast on the grid and close for 25 minutes.
6. Reduce the temperature to 375°F and roast for 20 minutes.
7. Generously brush the glaze on the roast and continue cooking for 10 minutes.
8. Brush the roast again and cook 10 minutes more. Continue the process until the internal temperature reaches 155°F.
9. Remove the roast from the grill and allow it to rest for 15 minutes before carving.

Caribbean St. Louis Style Ribs

Servings: 6
Cooking Time: 300 Minutes

Ingredients:

- 2 racks (about 4 pounds) St. Louis Style Ribs
- 2 cups Chipotle Mango Lime Sauce
- 1 cup Habanero Rub
- 2 cups wood chips, soaked for 30 minutes in water
- 1/2 cup olive oil
- 1/4 cup lime juice

Directions:

1. Combine olive oil, lime juice, and Habanero Rub. Set aside.
2. Rinse the spare ribs under cold water and pat-dry with a paper towel.
3. Put them on a cutting board, bone side up.
4. Remove the membrane and the flap of meat running along the entire length of the ribs.
5. After trimming, generously apply rub, olive oil, and lime juice mixture.
6. Grilling:
7. Let it sit at room temperature while preheat the grill to 225°F using direct heat with a cast iron grate installed.
8. Add wood chips, put the plate setter in place, and place the grid on top.
9. Set the ribs on the grid, bone side down.
10. Close the dome and allow the ribs to smoke for 3 hours.
11. Brush the ribs with Chipotle Mango Lime Sauce and close the dome for another hour, or until the internal temperature reaches 185°F.
12. Once done, remove from the smoker and allow to cool for 15 minutes before carving.
13. Serve with more sauce on the side.

Reuben Riffel's Yellow Bellied Pork

Servings:4
Cooking Time: 130 Minutes

Ingredients:

- 1⁄2 pork belly, deboned, fat scored finely
- 3 tbsp (45 ml) coarse salt
- 4 sprigs fresh thyme
- 1 1⁄2 cups (360 ml) curry sauce
- 8 dried apricots
- 1 cup (240 ml) water
- 1 cup (240 ml) sugar
- 2 star anise
- 2 tsp (10 ml) ground cinnamon
- 1 tbsp (15 ml) vegetable oil
- 2 medium onions, chopped
- 1⁄2 cup (120 ml) white wine vinegar
- 1 tsp (5 ml) garlic, chopped
- 1 tsp (5 ml) ginger, chopped
- 2 tbsp (30 ml) curry powder
- 2 tbsp (30 ml) garam masala
- 1 tbsp (15 ml) turmeric
- 1 tbsp (15 ml) paprika
- 3 allspice/pimentos
- 2 bay leaves
- 1 cup (240 ml) whole peeled tomatoes
- 1 cup (240 ml) water
- 1 cup (240 ml) chicken stock
- 1⁄2 cup (120 ml) sugar
- 1 tsp (5 ml) salt
- 1 tsp (5 ml) ground black pepper

Directions:

1. Rub the pork belly evenly with salt, focusing on the fatty part. Rub in the thyme evenly. Let cure for 30 minutes.

2. Preheat the grill to 325°F using direct heat with a cast iron grate installed. Place a drip pan on the platesetter and then add the stainless steel grid.

3. Dust the excess salt off the pork belly and add to the cooking grid, fatty side up. Cook for one hour and 40 minutes; flipping the meat over halfway through. Remove from the heat and let rest for 10 minutes before slicing. Serve drizzled with warm curry sauce and poached apricots.

4. Bring all the ingredients except the apricots to a boil. Turn down to a simmer, add the apricots and poach for two to three minutes. Remove from the heat and strain.

5. Set the kamado grill for direct cooking (without the platesetter) at 350°F.

6. Add the oil to a Stir-Fry & Paella Pan and cook the onions and spices until soft and fragrant. Deglaze the onion mixture with white wine vinegar and reduce the kamado grill temperature to 300°F.

7. Add the rest of the ingredients and cook for 20 to 30 minutes, or until the sauce has thickened to a thick gravy consistency. Blend until smooth and strain.

BURGERS

Breakfast Burger

Servings: 4
Cooking Time: 13 Minutes

Ingredients:
- 1 1/2 lb ground beef
- 1/2 lb ground pork breakfast sausage
- 2 Tablespoon butter
- 8 strips bacon
- 4 slices sharp cheddar cheese
- 4 Brioche buns
- 4 eggs
- 4 thick slices tomato

Directions:
1. In a medium bowl, mix ground beef and sausage until just combined.
2. Form into 4 patties and refrigerate while the grill heats.
3. Melt butter in a large skillet and fry the eggs for 2 minutes on each side.
4. Grilling:
5. Preheat the grill to 400°F using direct heat with a cast iron grate installed.
6. Place bacon on a small cookie sheet and place on the grid in the grill. Cook until crispy.
7. Place the patties on the grid and close the dome for 3 minutes.
8. Flip the burgers and replace the dome for an additional 3 minutes.
9. Close all of the vents and allow the burgers to sit for an additional 5 minutes. The internal temperature of the burger should be 150°F.
10. Place cheese on top of the burgers and cover for 1 more minute.
11. Assemble the burgers by placing a burger on the bottom bun, topping with bacon, tomato, and a fried egg.

Classic American Burger

Servings: 4
Cooking Time: 12 Minutes

Ingredients:
- 2 lbs ground beef
- 1/2 tsp salt
- 1/4 tsp pepper
- 4 slices American cheese
- 4 hamburger buns
- Green Leaf Lettuce
- Sliced Tomato
- Ketchup
- Mustard
- Sliced Pickle

Directions:
1. Form ground beef into four patties and season both sides with salt and pepper.
2. Grilling:
3. Preheat the grill to 500°F using direct heat with a cast iron grate installed.
4. Place burgers on the grid and close the dome for 3 minutes.
5. Flip burgers and close the dome for 2 more minutes.
6. Close all of the vents and allow the burgers to sit for 5 minutes.
7. Top each burger with a slice of cheese and close the dome for 1 more minute.
8. Build burgers with lettuce, tomato, pickle, mustard, and ketchup.

Oahu Burger

Servings: 4
Cooking Time: 12 Minutes

Ingredients:
- 2 lbs ground beef
- 1/4 cup thickened Teriyaki Marinade
- 1/4 cup mayonnaise
- 1/2 tsp sambal or sriracha
- 4 slices fresh pineapple, cored
- 4 slices tomato
- 4 slices butter lettuce
- 4 Hawaiian hamburger buns

Directions:
1. Form ground beef into four patties and season both sides with salt and pepper.
2. In a small bowl, mix mayonnaise with hot chile sauce and spread on buns.
3. Top each bun with a burger, slice of pineapple, lettuce and tomato.
4. Grilling:
5. Preheat the grill to 500°F using direct heat with a cast iron grate installed.
6. Place burgers on the grid and close the dome for 3 minutes.
7. Flip burgers, baste with Teriyaki Marinade, and place the pineapple slices on the grid. Close the dome for 2 more minutes.
8. Flip the burgers again and baste with remaining Teriyaki Marinade. Close the dome.
9. Close all of the vents and allow the burgers to sit for 5 minutes.

Quesadilla Burger

Servings: 4
Cooking Time: 12 Minutes

Ingredients:
- 2 lbs ground beef
- 2 Tablespoons Adobo Rub
- 1 cup shredded cheddar cheese
- 4 large flour tortillas
- Sour Cream
- Guacamole
- Salsa

Directions:
1. Form ground beef into four patties and season both sides with Adobo Rub.
2. Serve each burger with sour cream, guacamole, and salsa.
3. Grilling:
4. Preheat the grill to 500°F using direct heat with a cast iron grate installed.
5. Place burgers on the grid and close the dome for 3 minutes.
6. Flip burgers and close the dome for 2 more minutes.
7. Close all of the vents and allow the burgers to sit for 5 minutes.
8. Remove burgers and place flour tortillas on the grid.
9. Top each tortilla with shredded cheese and close the dome for 1 minute until the cheese melts.
10. Place a hamburger in the center of each tortilla and begin folding the tortilla around the burger like an envelope.

The Crowned Jewels Burger

Servings: 4
Cooking Time: 12 Minutes

Ingredients:
- 2 lbs ground beef
- 1/2 tsp salt
- 1/4 tsp pepper
- 1 lb thinly sliced pastrami
- 1 cup shredded Romaine lettuce
- 1/4 cup mayonnaise
- 2 Tablespoons ketchup
- 1/8 tsp onion powder
- 4 slices Sharp Cheddar cheese
- 4 hamburger buns
- 1 tomato, sliced

Directions:
1. Form ground beef into four patties and season both sides with salt and pepper.
2. Meanwhile, mix together mayonnaise, ketchup, and onion powder. Smear on each bun.
3. Place each pastrami and cheese covered burger on the prepared buns and top with shredded lettuce and tomato.
4. Grilling:
5. Preheat the grill to 500°F using direct heat with a cast iron grate installed.
6. Place burgers on the grid and close the dome for 3 minutes.
7. Flip burgers and close the dome for 2 more minutes.
8. Close all of the vents and allow the burgers to sit for 5 minutes.
9. Top each burger with 1/4 of the pastrami and a slice of cheese and close the dome for 1 more minute.

"the Masterpiece"

Servings: 4
Cooking Time: 12 Minutes

Ingredients:

- 2 lbs ground beef
- 6 ounces sliced mushrooms
- 4 Tablespoons shredded smoked Gouda
- 2 Tablespoons butter
- 2 Tablespoons olive oil
- 2 Tablespoons Dijon mustard
- 1/2 tsp salt
- 1/4 tsp pepper
- 8 slices bacon, cooked and crumbled
- 4 slices Swiss cheese
- 4 brioche buns
- 1 small onion, sliced

Directions:

1. Heat a skillet over medium heat and add 1 Tablespoon butter and 1 Tablespoon olive oil.
2. Place mushrooms in the pan and DO NOT MOVE THEM. Saute for 5-7 minutes or until the mushrooms are browned. Remove from the pan and set aside.
3. In the same skillet, heat remaining butter and olive oil and add onions. Saute over medium heat until they become translucent and begin to brown, about 10 minutes. Remove from the heat and set aside to cool.
4. Mix onion, mushrooms, and crumbled bacon.
5. Grilling:
6. Preheat the grill to 425°F using direct heat with a cast iron grate installed.
7. Form ground beef into eight patties and season both sides with salt and pepper.
8. Place a generous spoonful of the mushroom and onion mixture in the center of four patties and top with smoked Gouda.
9. Top with additional patty and press sides to seal the mixture inside.
10. Place burgers on the grid and close the dome for 5 minutes.
11. Flip burgers and close the dome for 3 more minutes.
12. Close all of the vents and allow the burgers to sit for 5 minutes.
13. Top each burger with a slice of Swiss cheese and close the dome for 1 more minute.
14. Spread buns with mustard, top with burgers and bun tops.

DESSERTS

Lemon Poppy Seed Cake

Servings: 10
Cooking Time: 45 Minutes

Ingredients:

- 1 tsp poppy seeds
- 2 lemons, zested and juiced
- 1 vanilla cake mix prepared according to package directions, substituting melted butter for oil and buttermilk for water
- 1 lb powdered sugar
- 4 ounces cream cheese
- 1 stick butter, softened
- 1/2 tsp vanilla
- 1/2 tsp lemon extract
- The juice and zest of 1 lemon

Directions:

1. Prepare cake mix according to package directions, substituting melted butter for the oil and buttermilk for the water.
2. Add the lemon zest, lemon juice, and poppy seeds.
3. Line the dutch oven with a liner.
4. Pour prepare cake mix into the liner and cover.
5. Grilling:
6. Preheat the grill to 350°F using direct heat with a cast iron grate installed.
7. Place the dutch oven on the grid and lower the dome for 30-40 minutes or until a toothpick inserted into the center comes out clean.
8. Meanwhile, combine glaze ingredients, adding milk to thin out the glaze if necessary.
9. Remove the cake from the grill and set aside to cool for 10 minutes before pouring glaze over the cake.
10. Serve warm.

Honey Whole Wheat Bread

Servings: 2
Cooking Time: 30 Minutes

Ingredients:

- 1 1/2 cups water
- 2 1/4 cups bread flour
- 3/4 cups whole wheat flour
- 2 Tablespoons honey
- 1 1/2 tsp salt
- 1 1/2 tsp yeast Directions:
- In a large bowl with a lid, combine water and honey until the honey is dissolved.
- In a separate bowl, combine flours, salt, and yeast.
- Stir the dry ingredients into the wet ingredients until well combined. DO NOT KNEAD.
- Allow the dough to sit in a warm, dry place until it doubles in size, about 30 minutes.
- Refrigerate the dough for 1 hour or up to 3 days.
- Remove the dough from the fridge and form half into a round loaf.
- Place a sheet of parchment paper in the bottom of the dutch oven and place the loaf on top.
- Grilling:
- Preheat the grill to 425°F using direct heat with a cast iron grate installed.
- Score the top of the loaf with an "X", cover, and place the dutch oven on the grid.
- Lower the dome for 30 minutes.
- Carefully remove the loaf from the dutch oven and allow it to cool before slicing.

Death By Chocolate

Servings: 8

Cooking Time: 60 Minutes

Ingredients:

- 1 chocolate cake mix, prepared according to package directions
- 2 cups chocolate chips
- 1 cup brown sugar
- 1 1/2 cups water
- 1/2 cup cocoa powder
- 1 (10 oz) bag miniature marshmallows

Directions:

1. Prepare cake mix according to package instructions.
2. Line the dutch oven with a liner.
3. In a medium bowl, combine water, brown sugar, and cocoa powder.
4. Pour the mixture into the bottom of the dutch oven.
5. Top with miniature marshmallows
6. Pour prepared cake mix on top.
7. Top with chocolate chips.
8. Grilling:
9. Preheat the grill to 350°F using direct heat with a cast iron grate installed.
10. Place the lid on the dutch oven and set on the grid of the grill.
11. Close the dome for 1 hour.
12. Remove the dutch oven from the grill, uncover, and serve warm.

3 Ingredient Fruit Cobbler

Servings: 8
Cooking Time: 30 Minutes

Ingredients:

- 1 stick butter, sliced
- 2 (29 oz) cans fruit, drained but reserving 1/2 cup of the liquid
- 1 yellow cake mix

Directions:

1. Line the dutch oven with a liner
2. Pour fruit into the bottom of the dutch oven with 1/2 cup of reserved liquid
3. Sprinkle the top with cake mix
4. Dot the top with butter.
5. Grilling:
6. Preheat the grill to 350°F using direct heat with a cast iron grate installed.
7. Cover the dutch oven and place on the grid of the grill.
8. Lower the dome for 30 minutes.
9. Allow the cobbler to sit for 10 minutes off the heat before serving.

4 Ingredient, No Knead Bread

Servings: 4
Cooking Time: 30 Minutes

Ingredients:

- 3 cups warm water
- 1 1/2 Tablespoons yeast
- 1 1/2 Tablespoons salt
- 6 1/2 cups bread flour

Directions:

1. In a 4-quart ice cream container, mix all ingredients until they come together. DO NOT KNEAD.
2. Cover, but do not seal the container and allow it to sit in a warm, dry place until it doubles in size, about 30 minutes.
3. Seal the container and place in the fridge for 1 hour.
4. Place a sheet of parchment paper in the bottom of the dutch oven.
5. Pinch off 1/4 of the dough and form into a ball.
6. Place the ball on the parchment paper and allow it to rest while the grill heats.
7. Grilling:
8. Preheat the grill to 425°F using direct heat with a cast iron grate installed.
9. Score the top of the dough ball with an "X".
10. Cover the dutch oven and place it on the grid of the grill.
11. Lower the Dome for 30 minutes.
12. Remove the bread from the dutch oven and allow it to cool before slicing.

Grilled Pineapple Sundaes

Servings: 4
Cooking Time: 5 Minutes

Ingredients:
- 4 fresh pineapple spears
- Vanilla Ice Cream
- Jarred Caramel Sauce
- Toasted Coconut

Directions:
1. Place pineapple spears on a 400°F grill and close the dome for 2 minutes.
2. Turn the pineapple and close the dome for another 2 minutes.
3. Turn the pineapple once more and close the dome for another minute.
4. Assembly:
5. Serve pineapple topped with ice cream, caramel sauce, and toasted coconut.

Orange Scented Vanilla Cake

Servings: 12
Cooking Time: 30 Minutes

Ingredients:

- 12 oranges
- 1/2 stick of butter
- 1 vanilla cake mix, prepared according to package instructions
- 1/2 lb of powdered sugar

Directions:

1. Cut the tops off of the oranges and, using a spoon, scoop out the insides of the orange. Eat the insides of the orange while you wait for the cake to cook.
2. Pour 1/3 of a cup of batter into each orange, replace the top and wrap with heavy duty aluminum foil.
3. In a separate bowl, combine butter, powdered sugar, and 2 Tablespoon orange juice.
4. When cakes are ready, drizzle some of the glaze over top of each cake and serve inside the orange.
5. Grilling:
6. Place the oranges on a 350°F grill for 30 minutes or until the cake is done.

Caramel Cinnamon Rolls

Servings: 4

Cooking Time: 30 Minutes

Ingredients:

- 18 frozen cinnamon rolls, thawed (you can also used canned cinnamon rolls)
- 1/2 cup brown sugar
- 1/2 cup graham cracker crumbs
- 1/2 cup caramel ice cream topping
- 1 tsp cinnamon

Directions:

1. Line the dutch oven with a liner.
2. Cut each cinnamon roll into 4 pieces and arrange them around the bottom of the dutch oven.
3. In a separate bowl, combine brown sugar, graham cracker crumbs, and cinnamon.
4. Sprinkle some of the mixture over the layer of cinnamon rolls. Repeat.
5. Grilling:
6. Preheat the grill to 350°F using direct heat with a cast iron grate installed.
7. Cover the dutch oven and place it on the grid of the grill.
8. Lower the dome for 25-30 minutes or until the cinnamon rolls are golden brown.
9. Drizzle caramel ice cream topping over the warm rolls and serve.

Chocolate Cake

Servings: 12
Cooking Time: 45 Minutes

Ingredients:

- 2 cups all-purpose flour
- 2 cups sugar
- 2/3 cup cocoa powder
- 2 tsp baking soda
- 1 tsp baking powder
- 1 tsp kosher salt
- 2 large eggs, at room temperature
- 1 cup buttermilk, at room temperature
- 1 cup strong black coffee, warm
- 1/2 cup vegetable oil
- 1 tbsp pure vanilla extract
- flaky sea salt, for topping (optional)
- for the caramel sauce
- 3/4 cup sugar
- 4 tbsp water
- 4 tsp light corn syrup
- 1/4 cup heavy cream
- 1 tsp pure vanilla extract
- 11/2 tbsp unsalted butter
- for the frosting
- 12 tbsp unsalted butter, at room temperature
- 21/2 cups powdered sugar
- 1 tsp pure vanilla extract
- 1 tbsp heavy cream
- kosher salt

Directions:

1. Preheat the grill to 350°F (177°C) using indirect heat with a standard grate installed. Grease a 9-in (23-cm) round metal cake pan with nonstick cooking spray and line with parchment paper. (Instead of a cake pan, you can also use a well-seasoned dutch oven.)

2. In a large bowl or the bowl of a stand mixer, sift together flour, sugar, cocoa powder, baking soda, baking powder, and salt. In a separate medium bowl, whisk together eggs, buttermilk, coffee, vegetable oil, and vanilla extract.

3. Gradually add the liquid ingredients to the dry ingredients, stopping to scrape the sides and bottom of the bowl, until just combined. (The batter will be thin.) Pour the batter into the prepared cake pan or dutch oven. Place on the grate, close the grill lid, and bake until a toothpick inserted in the center comes out almost clean, about 25 to 30 minutes. Let sit for 5 minutes, then turn out onto a wire rack to cool completely. (Use a butter knife to loosen the edges if needed.)

4. To make the caramel sauce, in a small saucepan, combine sugar, water, and corn syrup. Place on the stovetop over medium heat, and simmer until the mixture is deep amber in color, about 10 to 15 minutes. Slowly and carefully, add heavy cream, whisking constantly, then whisk in vanilla, butter, and a pinch of salt.

5. To make the frosting, in the bowl of a stand mixer fitted with the paddle attachment, beat butter on medium speed until light and fluffy, about 2 to 3 minutes. Add sugar, vanilla extract, heavy cream, and a pinch of salt. Beat on low speed until combined, about 1 minute. Increase the speed to medium-high and beat for 6 minutes. Add 1/2 cup caramel sauce and mix until combined.

6. Spread the frosting evenly over top and sides of the cooled cake, and drizzle with caramel sauce. Sprinkle with flaky sea salt (if desired) before serving.

Upside Down Triple Berry Pie

Servings: 8
Cooking Time: 35 Minutes

Ingredients:
- 6 cups frozen triple berry mix
- 2 Tablespoons lemon juice
- 1 refrigerated pie crust
- 1 cup sugar, divided
- 4 Tablespoons cornstarch

Directions:
1. Place a liner in the dutch oven.
2. In a separate bowl, combine frozen berries with 3/4 cup sugar, cornstarch, and lemon juice.
3. Pour berries into the bottom of the lined dutch oven.
4. Unroll pie crust and place on top of berry mixture.
5. Cut 4 vent holes into the crust.
6. Sprinkle remaining sugar over the pie crust.
7. Grilling:
8. Preheat the grill to 425°F using direct heat with a cast iron grate installed.
9. Cover the dutch oven and place on the grid.
10. Lower the dome for 35 minutes or until the crust is golden and the berry mixture has thickened.
11. Cut the crust as you would any pie.
12. Serve a piece of crust topped with ice cream and a scoop of the thickened berry mixture.

Peach Dutch Baby

Servings: 8
Cooking Time: 25 Minutes

Ingredients:

- 8 oz frozen peaches, thawed (or 3 ripe peaches, peeled and sliced)
- 1 cup whole milk
- 4 eggs
- 1 cup flour
- 1/4 cup sugar
- 1/4 cup butter
- 1 tsp vanilla
- 1 tsp cinnamon
- 1/2 tsp salt

Directions:

1. In a blender, combine milk, flour, sugar, vanilla, cinnamon, salt, and eggs until smooth.
2. Grilling:
3. Preheat the grill to 425°F using direct heat with a cast iron grate installed.
4. Place the dutch oven on the grid of the grill and melt the butter.
5. Line the bottom of the pot with peaches and pour over milk and egg mixture.
6. Close the dome for 20 minutes or until the top of the Dutch Baby is golden brown.
7. Serve with a sprinkling of powdered sugar.

Grilled Plums With Honey And Ricotta

Servings: 4

Cooking Time: 5 Minutes

Ingredients:
- 4 plums, cut in half and pitted
- 1/2 cup whole milk ricotta cheese
- 2 Tablespoons honey
- 1/4 tsp cracked black pepper

Directions:
1. Place the plums, cut side down on a 400°F grill.
2. Close the dome for 5 minutes.
3. Assembly:
4. Serve the plums, cut side up, with a dollop of ricotta, a drizzle of honey, and a sprinkling of cracked black pepper.

Grilled Sopapillas

Servings: 6
Cooking Time: 18 Minutes

Ingredients:
- 1 pizza dough, divided into 6 pieces
- 3 Tablespoons melted butter
- 1/4 cup sugar
- 1 Tablespoon cinnamon

Directions:
1. Stretch dough into round shape.
2. Place the dough directly on the pizza stone in a 500°F grill.
3. Brush with melted butter and top with cinnamon sugar.
4. Close the dome for 3 minutes, then remove.
5. Repeat with remaining dough.

Triple Berry Crostata

Servings: 8
Cooking Time: 50 Minutes

Ingredients:
- 1 1/2 cups all-purpose flour
- 11 Tablespoons butter, cut into 1/2 inch cubes
- 3 Tablespoons whole milk
- 2 tsp sugar
- 1 large egg yolk
- 2 cups frozen triple berry blend
- 1/4 cup sugar
- 2 Tablespoons cornstarch

Directions:
1. In a food processor, combine flour and butter and pulse until pea-sized cubes of butter can be seen throughout the flour.
2. Add sugar, egg yolk, and milk and pulse until the dough comes together.
3. Form the dough into a circle, cover tightly with plastic wrap, and refrigerate 20 minutes.
4. Roll the dough into a large round and place on a pizza peel covered in cornmeal.
5. In a bowl, combine fruit, sugar, and cornstarch and pile into the center of the dough.
6. Beginning on one side, fold the dough 1/3 of the way over the fruit, repeating until a free-form tart is formed.
7. Grilling:
8. Preheat the grill to 350°F using direct heat with a cast iron grate installed.
9. Slide the crostata onto the pizza stone and close the dome for 40-55 minutes or until the crust is golden brown.
10. Remove the crostata from the grill and allow to cool slightly before slicing and serving.

SIDES

Grilled Vegetable & Couscous Salad

Servings: 6
Cooking Time: 30 Minutes

Ingredients:
- 1 small zucchini, halved
- 1 small yellow squash, halved
- 1/2 red onion
- 6 sun-dried tomatoes
- 1 tbsp olive oil
- 2 cups uncooked Israeli couscous
- 4 cups vegetable stock, heated
- 4 basil leaves, stacked, rolled, and cut crosswise into thin strips, plus more to garnish
- 2 tbsp coarsely chopped fresh flat-leaf parsley, plus more to garnish
- for the marinade
- 1/4 cup balsamic vinegar
- 1/2 tsp Dijon mustard
- 1 garlic clove, coarsely chopped
- 1/2 cup olive oil
- kosher salt and freshly ground black pepper

Directions:

1. To make the marinade, in a small bowl, whisk together vinegar, mustard, and garlic. Slowly add oil, whisking until combined. Season with salt and pepper to taste.

2. Place zucchini, yellow squash, onion, and sun-dried tomatoes in a shallow dish. Pour half the marinade over the vegetables, toss to coat, and let sit at room temperature for 15 minutes. Cover the remaining marinade and set aside.

3. Preheat the grill to 400°F (204°C) with a cast iron grate installed and a dutch oven on the grate. Remove the vegetables from the marinade and place on the grate around the dutch oven. Close the lid and grill until beginning to soften and char, about 7 to 10 minutes. Transfer the vegetables to a cutting board and cut into bite-sized pieces. Set aside.

4. In the hot dutch oven, heat oil until shimmering. Add couscous, and toast until lightly golden brown, about 2 minutes. Add vegetable stock until couscous is just covered (add hot water if more liquid is needed to cover), close the grill lid, and bring to a boil. Cook until firm to the bite, about 7 to 10 minutes, and drain well.

5. Spoon the couscous into a large serving bowl and add the grilled vegetables, basil, and parsley. Drizzle the reserved marinade over top, and toss well to coat. Serve at room temperature with more basil and parsley to garnish.

Breakfast Casserole

Servings: 6
Cooking Time: 40 Minutes

Ingredients:

- 1 lb bulk pork breakfast sausage
- 1 (16 oz) bag of frozen O'Brien style hash browns
- 1 dozen eggs, beaten
- 1/4 cup grated onion
- 1/4 tsp black pepper
- Hot sauce for garnish

Directions:

1. Preheat the grill to 350°F using direct heat with a cast iron grate installed with the dutch oven on the grid.
2. Brown sausage with onion in the dutch oven.
3. Add hash browns and stir to combine.
4. Add eggs and cover.
5. Lower the dome for 15 minutes or until the eggs are just cooked through.
6. Serve the casserole with hot sauce for garnish.

Thanksgiving Stuffing

Servings: 8
Cooking Time: 45 Minutes

Ingredients:
- 8 ounces bulk breakfast sausage
- 4 cups cornbread, crumbled
- 4 cups sourdough bread, cut in cubes
- 1/2 cup onion, diced
- 1/2 cup celery, diced
- 1/2 cup Granny Smith apple, diced
- 4 Tablespoons butter, softened
- 2 cups chicken broth
- 1 tsp poultry seasoning

Directions:
1. Preheat the grill to 375°F using direct heat with a cast iron grate installed with the dutch oven on the grid.
2. Cook breakfast sausage in the dutch oven until brown.
3. Add onion and celery and cook until soft, about 5 minutes.
4. Add apple and cook an additional 2 minutes.
5. Stir in crumbled cornbread and sourdough bread cubes.
6. Pour chicken broth over mixture and season with poultry seasoning.
7. Dot the top of the stuffing with butter, cover, and lower the dome.
8. Cook the stuffing for 30 minutes. Serve warm.

Grilled Polenta

Servings: 8
Cooking Time: 5 Minutes

Ingredients:

- 3 cups water
- 3/4 cups parmesan cheese, grated
- 2 Tablespoons butter
- 1 tsp fresh thyme, chopped
- 1 1/2 cups quick cooking polenta
- 2 tsp salt
- 1 tsp pepper
- Olive oil for brushing

Directions:

1. In a large pot, bring water to a boil with the salt.
2. Slowly whisk in polenta and season with pepper.
3. Continue to whisk until polenta becomes firm.
4. Stir in parmesan and thyme.
5. Pour polenta into a buttered 10 inch springform pan and refrigerate for 1 1/2 - 2 hours or until the polenta is firm.
6. Remove the polenta from the springform pan and slice into 8 pieces.
7. Grilling:
8. Brush both sides with olive oil and place on a 400°F grill.
9. Close the dome and cook for 2 minutes.
10. Turn the polenta, close the dome and continue to cook for another 2 minutes. Serve warm.

Smoked Potato Salad

Servings: 8
Cooking Time: 120 Minutes

Ingredients:

- 4 large baking potatoes
- 4 large eggs, hard boiled and finely chopped
- 2 green onions, finely chopped
- 2 large dill pickles, finely chopped
- 1 rib celery, finely diced
- 1/2 cup mayonnaise
- The juice of 1 lemon
- 1/2 tsp black pepper
- 1/2 tsp celery seed
- 1/2 tsp dried dill

Directions:

1. Scrub the potatoes.
2. Grilling:
3. Place the potatoes alongside meat that is smoking at 225°F.
4. Assembly:
5. When the potatoes are fork tender, chill in the refrigerator for 30 minutes.
6. Peel and cut potatoes into small cubes.
7. In a large bowl, combine dressing ingredients.
8. Add potatoes, eggs, green onion, pickle, and celery to the dressing and gently toss

Mac And Cheese

Servings: 6
Cooking Time: 60 Minutes

Ingredients:

- 1 lb smoked cheddar cheese, shredded, divided
- 1/4 cup butter
- 2 eggs
- 1/2 lb elbow macaroni
- 3/4 cups evaporated milk
- 1/4 cup Panko breadcrumbs
- 1 tsp salt
- 3/4 tsp dry mustard

Directions:

1. In a large pot of boiling, salted water cook the macaroni according to package directions and drain.
2. In a separate bowl, whisk together the eggs, milk, hot sauce, salt, pepper, and mustard.
3. Grilling:
4. Preheat the grill to 350°F using direct heat with a cast iron grate installed with the dutch oven on the grid.
5. Melt the butter in the dutch oven and place macaroni in the pot. Toss to coat.
6. Stir the egg and milk mixture into the pasta and add half of the cheese.
7. Continuously stir the mac and cheese for 3 minutes or until creamy.
8. Top with remaining cheese and Panko breadcrumbs.
9. Cover the dutch oven, lower the dome, and cook for 20-25 minutes.
10. Serve immediately.

Asiago & Sage Scalloped Potatoes

Servings: 10
Cooking Time: 60 Minutes

Ingredients:

- 2 tbsp unsalted butter
- 2 medium yellow onions, thinly sliced
- 1/2 tsp finely chopped garlic
- 2 bay leaves
- 1/4 tsp grated fresh nutmeg
- 1 tbsp kosher salt
- 3/4 tsp ground black pepper
- 11/4 cups heavy cream
- 1/2 cup whole milk
- 2 tbsp finely chopped fresh sage
- 21/2lb (1.1kg) Idaho potatoes, peeled and thinly sliced
- for the topping
- 1 cup freshly grated Asiago cheese, about 3oz (85g) in total
- 1 cup plain breadcrumbs
- 2 tbsp extra virgin olive oil
- 1/4 tsp kosher salt
- 1/4 tsp ground black pepper
- 11/2 tsp finely chopped fresh sage

Directions:

1. Preheat the grill to 400°F (204°C) using indirect heat with a standard grate installed. Place a large heavy-bottomed saucepan on the grate and melt butter. Add onions, close the lid, and grill until golden brown, about 8 minutes, stirring often.

2. Add garlic, bay leaves, nutmeg, salt, and pepper, and cook for 30 seconds. Add heavy cream and milk, and bring to a boil. Remove from the heat, cover, and let sit for 5 minutes. Remove bay leaves and stir in sage.

3. To make the topping, in a medium bowl, toss cheese with breadcrumbs, olive oil, salt, pepper, and sage.

4. In a large bowl, gently toss potatoes with the onion mixture. Spread half the potatoes and liquid in a 2-quart (2-liter) grill-safe baking dish and sprinkle 2⁄3 cup of the cheese and breadcrumb mixture over top. Add the remaining potatoes to the dish, pressing firmly to pack them down. Spoon any remaining liquid over the potatoes and cover with the remaining breadcrumbs.

5. Place the dish on the grate, close the grill lid, and cook until potatoes are fork tender and the top is golden brown, about 1 hour. (If the top browns too quickly, loosely cover the dish with aluminum foil). Remove potatoes from the grill and serve hot.

Broiled Tomatoes And Parmesan

Servings: 4

Cooking Time: 5 Minutes

Ingredients:

- 1/4 cup parmesan, shredded
- 4 roma tomatoes
- 1 Tablespoon olive oil
- 1 tsp red wine vinegar
- Salt & Pepper

Directions:

1. Cut each tomato in half, lengthwise, and brush with olive oil.
2. Grilling:
3. Preheat the grill to 500°F using direct heat with a cast iron grate installed and lower the dome for 2 minutes.
4. Turn the tomatoes, season with vinegar, salt, and pepper and top with parmesan cheese.
5. Lower the dome for an additional 2 minutes or until the cheese melts. Serve warm.

Mojito Watermelon

Servings: 8
Cooking Time: 5 Minutes

Ingredients:

- 2 slices watermelon, 1 inch thick
- 1 lime, halved
- 2 Tablespoons mint, julienned
- 1 tsp honey
- 1/2 tsp salt

Directions:

1. Grilling:
2. Place the lime halves, cut side down, on a 500°F grill for 5 minutes.
3. Assembly:
4. Cut the watermelon slices into 8 pie-shaped pieces.
5. Squeeze grilled limes over watermelon.
6. Sprinkle the watermelon with salt, drizzle with honey, and top with mint.

German Potato Salad

Servings: 8
Cooking Time: 70 Minutes

Ingredients:

- 2lb (1kg) Yukon Gold potatoes, unpeeled and cut into rounds or bite-sized pieces
- 1/2lb (225g) thick-cut bacon
- 3/4 cup finely chopped yellow onion
- 1/3 cup white vinegar
- 1/4 cup sugar
- 1 tbsp Dijon mustard
- 1 tsp kosher salt
- 2 tbsp minced chives, to garnish

Directions:

1. Preheat the grill to 350ºF (177°C) using indirect heat with a cast iron grate installed and a cast iron skillet on the grate. Place potatoes on the grate around the skillet, close the lid, and roast until fork tender, about 45 minutes. Remove potatoes from the grill and set aside.
2. Add bacon to the hot skillet, close the lid, and cook until crisp, about 10 to 15 minutes. Once crisp, transfer to a plate lined with a paper towel and crumble into small pieces. Pour off the rendered fat, reserving 4 tbsp in the skillet.
3. Add onion to the skillet, close the lid, and cook until translucent and beginning to brown, about 4 to 5 minutes. Whisk in vinegar, sugar, mustard, and salt, and stir until thick and bubbly, about 2 to 3 minutes. Add the cooked potatoes, and toss to coat.
4. Remove the skillet from the grill, top with crumbled bacon, and garnish with chives. Serve warm.

Grilled Endive Salad

Servings: 6
Cooking Time: 2 Minutes

Ingredients:

- 2 cups frisee
- 1/2 cup pecan halves
- 1/4 cup dried cranberries
- 1/4 cup crumbled bacon
- 2 heads endive
- 1 bunch spinach, cleaned and stems removed
- 1/4 cup olive oil
- 2 Tablespoons Dijon Mustard
- 1 Tablespoon honey
- 1 shallot, finely minced
- The juice of 1 lemon
- Kosher salt and fresh cracked pepper to taste

Directions:

1. In a large bowl, combine dressing ingredients. Set aside.
2. Grilling:
3. Split endive down the middle, lengthwise and preheat the grill to 425°F using direct heat with a cast iron grate installed.
4. Remove the endive and slice into half rounds.
5. Toss shredded frisee, sliced endive, spinach, pecans, and cranberries in the dressing and serve immediately.

Ratatouille

Servings: 4
Cooking Time: 30 Minutes

Ingredients:
- 1/2 cup fresh, shredded basil
- 2 cloves garlic, minced
- 2 large tomatoes, chopped
- 1 red bell pepper, chopped
- 1 large eggplant, peeled and cut into 1/2 inch cubes
- 1 onion, sliced thin
- 1/4 cup olive oil
- 1/4 tsp dried oregano
- 1/4 tsp dried thyme
- 1/4 tsp fennel seeds
- 3/4 tsp salt

Directions:
1. Preheat the grill to 350°F using direct heat with a cast iron grate installed with the dutch oven on the grid.
2. Add olive oil to the pot and toast oregano, thyme, and fennel for 1 minute.
3. Add onion and cook for 5 minutes or until the onion is soft.
4. Add remaining vegetables, cover, and lower the dome for 20-25 minutes.
5. Serve topped with basil.

Arroz A La Mexicana (mexican Rice)

Servings: 8

Cooking Time: 30 Minutes

Ingredients:

- 2 small white onions, peeled and halved
- 2 poblano peppers, left whole
- 2 carrots, peeled
- 1/4 cup vegetable oil
- 3 garlic cloves, minced
- 2 cups uncooked white rice
- 4 cups chicken stock
- 1/4 cup tomato paste
- 11/2 tbsp ground cumin
- 1 bunch of fresh cilantro, chopped

Directions:

1. Preheat the grill to 400ºF (204°C) using direct heat with a cast iron grate installed and a dutch oven on the grate. Place onions, peppers, and carrots on the grate around the dutch oven, close the lid, and grill until beginning to soften and char, about 7 to 10 minutes. Remove the vegetables from the grill, chop onions and peppers, and dice carrots into small cubes.
2. In the hot dutch oven, heat oil until shimmering. Add carrots, and cook for 2 minutes, stirring occasionally. Stir in onions and garlic, and cook for 1 minute, stirring occasionally. Add rice, stock, tomato paste, and cumin. Bring to a boil, stirring once or twice. Cover the dutch oven with its lid and close the grill lid. Cook until rice is tender and liquid is absorbed, about 15 minutes.
3. Remove the dutch oven from the grill, stir peppers and cilantro into the rice, and fluff the rice with a fork. Serve immediately.

Campfire Potato Salad

Servings: 10
Cooking Time: 10 Minutes

Ingredients:
- 2lb (1kg) new potatoes, unpeeled
- 1 green bell pepper, left whole
- 1 red bell pepper, left whole
- 1/2 red onion
- 1/4 cup mayonnaise
- 1/4 cup sour cream
- 1 tbsp Dijon mustard
- 3/4 tsp garlic, minced
- 1 tbsp kosher salt
- 1/4 tsp ground black pepper
- 1 tbsp chopped fresh dill
- 2 celery stalks, diced

Directions:
1. Preheat the grill to 425°F (218°C) using direct heat with a cast iron grate installed. Place potatoes, peppers, and onion on the grate, close the lid, and grill until beginning to soften and char, about 7 to 10 minutes, turning once or twice.
2. Remove the vegetables from the grill and let cool slightly. Cut the potatoes into quarters and dice the peppers and onion.
3. In a large bowl, combine mayonnaise, sour cream, mustard, garlic, salt, pepper, and dill. Add potatoes, peppers, onions, and celery to the mayonnaise mixture, and gently combine until the vegetables are evenly coated with the dressing. Taste and adjust the seasoning as needed. Serve warm.

RECIPES INDEX

Lightning Source UK Ltd.
Milton Keynes UK
UKHW051605070822
406949UK00004B/178